The U.S.S. *Wisconsin*:
A History of Two Battleships

The U.S.S. *Wisconsin*:
A History of Two Battleships

By Richard H. Zeitlin

With an essay on the ships' silver
By Anne Woodhouse

THE STATE HISTORICAL SOCIETY OF WISCONSIN
Madison • 1988

ACKNOWLEDGMENTS

I want to thank Captain Jerry M. Blesch, commanding officer of the U.S.S. *Wisconsin*, for his interest in the history and museum exhibit phase of the state's battleship commemorative program. Captain Blesch assigned Chief Warrant Officer Harry A. Curtis to help show me historical items relating to the ship. Curtis arranged meetings with representatives of Ingalls Shipbuilding, and introduced me to Robert C. Ballinger of the Navy Department's Battleship Program Office in Washington, who shared materials from his own collection of battleship memorabilia. I am likewise grateful to the former officers and crew of BB-64, Captains Earl E. Stone and H. C. Bruton foremost among them, for their helpful response to my inquiries about their service aboard ship.

Captain David M. Kletter of the Department of Naval Science at the University of Wisconsin–Madison helped overcome an unavoidable Navy bureaucratic tangle in record time. Lieutenant Terri L. Kaish of the Naval Office of Information in Chicago also deserves mention for her help with the project.

Staff members at the Naval Historical Center in Washington generously provided their assistance. John C. Reilly, Jr., of the Ships Histories Branch, Bernard Cavalcante and Mrs. Kathy Lloyd of the Center's Operational Archives, and Charles R. Haberlein, Jr., of the photographic section helped me use the precious research time I spent in Washington efficiently.

Professor Malcolm Muir of the U.S. Military Academy at West Point offered helpful suggestions which contributed to the research on *Wisconsin*. Muir's book, *The Iowa Class Battleships*, had just been published and he knew where to find useful files and interesting photographs. He also shared with me his insights regarding the recommissioning of the battleships.

Ms. Lynnette M. Wolfe, of the Wisconsin Veterans Museums, merits special thanks for her many contributions to the success of the project. No author ever had a more able or devoted assistant. Daniel Strizek's help was also greatly appreciated.

The cooperation of the State Historical Society of Wisconsin and the Wisconsin Department of Veterans Affairs made possible this history of the U.S.S. *Wisconsin*. Veterans Affairs Secretary John J. Maurer and State Historical Society Director Dr. H. Nicholas Muller III supported the project wholeheartedly, and I am most grateful to both of them.

RICHARD H. ZEITLIN
Curator
Wisconsin Veterans Museums
Madison, Wisconsin

Published by the State Historical Society of Wisconsin
in cooperation with the Wisconsin Department of Veterans Affairs
and the Governor's Commission on the U.S.S. Wisconsin.

GOVERNOR'S MESSAGE

As you are about to discover, the history of our state's namesake ships is a long and honorable one. It is a proud story that reflects Wisconsin's traditions in the defense of our country and constitution.

As we read this story, we would be well served to keep in mind the men and women who have given of themselves in that defense. They have left Wisconsin a proud legacy and remind us that powerful guns and magnificent ships mean little without people to serve them. Even in this short work, it becomes clear that in the end, it is human dedication to skill in duty and service, and devotion to country, that decides the outcome in the defense of freedom.

With this most recent recommissioning, Wisconsin will be renewing a tradition of a strong and ongoing relationship with the people who serve in her namesake ship and who maintain Wisconsin's continuing commitment to support the cause of peace, freedom, and democracy.

I join with all the people of Wisconsin in wishing them well and thanking them for a job well done.

TOMMY G. THOMPSON
Governor
State of Wisconsin

FOREWORD

In the early years of World War II, those of us deployed in the Western Pacific used to say "Golden Gate '48." This was the conventional wisdom about how long it would take to defeat the Japanese enemy.

Our thinking changed when the vast armada of new ships began to join us. What a beautiful sight it was to see those new splendid battleships with their impressive survivability and firepower. As a destroyer man, I helped to protect them from submarines and welcomed the protective umbrellas they provided throughout the balance of World War II.

When the Korean War broke out I had the thrill of being Navigator of U.S.S. *Wisconsin* (BB-64) and there came to appreciate even more her versatility, maneuverability, strength, and power. Now, over three decades later, the *Wisconsin* once more proudly rejoins the fleet to bring confidence and inspiration to a whole new generation of Navy men.

E. R. ZUMWALT, JR.
Admiral, U.S. Navy (Ret.)

The U.S.S. *Wisconsin*:
A History of Two Battleships

By Richard H. Zeitlin

To anyone with an interest in modern American history, the recommissioning of a battleship is a noteworthy event. These magnificent vessels continue their hold on the public's imagination long after being pronounced obsolete by experts, and forty-odd years after the last enemy battleship was sunk. And it is not only naval strategists and military buffs who follow their exploits. Let an American battleship stand off any shore in the world and it becomes front-page news. Let one make a call at a friendly port and thousands of tourists eagerly flock to visit a ship that exudes the unmistakable aura of strength. While aircraft carriers and missile-firing submarines are undoubtedly vessels of great importance, the battleship somehow epitomizes naval glamor. Historians remind us, after all, that it was the battleship more than any other military instrument that made the United States a world power.

Today only four battleships exist: the four World War II-era sister ships *Iowa*, *New Jersey*, *Missouri*, and *Wisconsin*, all of which underwent modernization and redevelopment between 1981 and 1988.* It therefore seems appropriate to commemorate the recommissioning of

the U.S.S. *Wisconsin* with a narrative tracing the ship's lineage and career at sea, to convey a sense of its size and complexity, and to place it in the historical context of twentieth-century arms and diplomacy.

EARLY BATTLESHIPS

BATTLESHIPS evolved over 300 years. Their predecessors included the large, heavy sailing ships of the sixteenth century, which grew in size and armament until they attained certain physical limits in the following century. Tactical deployment of these powerful men-of-war in linear formations led to their being classified as "ships of the line of battle," or ships of the line.

Veritable floating fortresses, ships of the line generally mounted between seventy-four and 120 cannons on two or three enclosed gun decks. They displaced about 4,000 tons, and had crews of nearly 1,000 men. Each ship of the line consumed about 3,500 full-grown oak trees for its construction, denuding some 900 acres of forest. Three masts coupled to square-rigged sails provided the ship with motive power, and because wind energy required no replenishment, such vessels had great range. Wooden walls nearly two feet thick protected crewmen in battle while contributing at the same time to the ships' structural integrity and buoyancy.

*Three other World War II battleships exist as museums or state memorials: U.S.S. *Alabama* (at Mobile); U.S.S. *Massachusetts* (at Fall River); and U.S.S. *North Carolina* (at Wilmington). The World War I-era battleship *Texas* is also a state memorial, at Houston.

The steam-powered wooden "super cruiser" U.S.S. Wampanoag, *completed in 1867,
was the fastest warship in the world for twenty years. From an oil painting by John
Charles Roach.*

prowess. Future naval conflicts, they believed, would be fought distantly, "at the threshold" rather "than upon our hearthstone."

The United States' hesitancy to adopt iron-clad seagoing ships made sense. Armor, as experience demonstrated, did not provide invulnerability to ships despite adding enormously to both their expense and their weight. The United States expected to be recognized as a powerful nation after the Civil War, but it had no desire to challenge the leading European powers outside the Western Hemisphere. The *Wampanoag*s and double-turreted monitors in combination did represent credible instruments of national defense, particularly when America's ability to raise huge land forces was considered.

Problems arose for the American Navy when both types of vessels were assigned secondary roles by resurgent conservatives who longed for a return to the days of sail. During the Reconstruction era, moreover, political corruption and bitter partisan battles completed the job of transforming the Navy into a collection of rotting hulks. Internal difficulties caused the United States to fall well behind other nations in the development of battle-ships.

THE DOLDRUMS

CONSERVATIVES rebelled against steam engineering after the Civil War. The highest-ranking American naval officer, Admiral David D. Porter, convinced the Secretary of the Navy in 1869 to order all U.S. vessels "fitted out with full sail power." Cruising would be carried out under sail power alone. High-speed propellers were scrapped in favor of ones which interfered least with a ship's sailing characteristics. Captains were required to report and to justify any use of auxiliary steam power. Coal consumption figures for ships of the Navy were recorded in red ink, and some suggested that commanding officers be personally required to pay for any coal their ships used. U.S.S. *Wampanoag*, the world's fastest warship, had half its boilers removed before being deactivated, and eventually she was sold as "naval trash."

Concern for fueling stations and the obvious lack of U.S. overseas bases for supplying steamships with coal contributed somewhat to the conservative longing for a return to the days of sail. But the anti-steam officers were, in fact, overly concerned with keeping their scrubbed decks clean, their billowy sails white, their cabin spaces ample, and maintaining antiquated sailing skills.

The post-Civil War Navy continued to rely upon cast-iron, muzzle-loading, and mostly smoothbore ordnance along with its wooden sailing ships. Meanwhile, spectacular advances in metallurgy, gun fabrication techniques, and the chemistry of propellants greatly multiplied the power of modern European ordnance. American warships, however, were not equipped with the long-barreled steel breech-loading rifled guns with their increased velocity, great range, and superior penetrating power. Indeed, no heavy ordnance was even produced in the United States until after 1885. An improved telescopic range-finding gun sight, of advanced design and manufactured by an American naval officer, was rejected by the United States. Foreign powers eagerly adopted the device to increase the accuracy and range of their own naval artillery.

In truth, the recoil effect alone of modern ordnance alone might have damaged wooden American ship hulls. A 12-inch breech-loading rifled cannon of the late nineteenth century, firing its 850-pound projectile with smokeless powder at 3,000 feet per second, for instance, generated a recoil force equivalent to that of halting a railroad engine moving at twenty miles an hour within three feet. This new breed of guns necessitated large iron (and later steel) ships, capable of mounting both the heavy weapons and thick armor to protect vessels from the shells of similarly equipped opponents. As the world's first-class capital warships—"battleships" as they came to be called—grew larger and more formidably armed, the American Navy dipped into obscurity.

From its 1865 peak of nearly 700 ships, the American Navy list fell to 200 ships (with only fifty-two in commission) five years later. In 1873, during a crisis involving Spain, the Navy listed forty-three ships as being fit for service—including fourteen single-turret, harbor-bound monitors. Only one American ship mounted rifled guns. Fleet maneuvers in 1874 were described as "lamentable." In 1880, thirty-eight admirals commanded a Navy of thirty-nine serviceable ships. The U.S. Navy ranked twelfth in the world, behind such nations as Holland, Brazil, China, and Chile.

Partisan politics and cronyism added to the Navy's woes. During the eight years of Ulysses S. Grant's administration, for example, the Secretary of the Navy distributed jobs in shipyards as rewards for party loyalty. Navy yards became active mainly during electoral campaigns. Funds earmarked for repairs seemed, unaccountably, to be rarely sufficient. Some Secretaries of the Navy knew little about ships

Even in a moderate sea, the decks of the double-turreted monitor U.S.S. Monadnock *were awash. From an 1898 photograph.*

U. S. Navy Historical Center

or their departments. Grant's appointee, for instance, was known primarily for his expert judgments concerning horses and trout fishing. The reform-minded Rutherford B. Hayes named a shrewd Indiana politician who had never seen the ocean to be his Secretary of the Navy. Upon visiting a ship for the first time, Secretary of the Navy Richard W. Thompson remarked, "Why bless me, the damned thing is hollow."

The Navy lacked a sense of purpose or direction. By the mid-1880's, even inertia-bound naval leaders began to admit that problems existed. Admiral Porter himself likened the Navy to "a Chinese fort upon which dragons are painted to frighten the enemy away."

Congress began taking steps to rectify the situation. European involvement in various Isthmian canal projects, growing U.S. foreign trade, and the realization that American naval power was insufficient to protect the nation in any way, even against South American opponents, encouraged congressional investigations and calls for improvement. During 1883, appropriations were made for the construction of three sail-rigged but steel-hulled cruisers and a dispatch ship all equipped with modern steam engines. Modern gun-manufacturing plants and a new armor industry date from 1885 when Congress directed that U.S. ships be produced from domestic materials. The birth of the "New Navy" can be dated from the recommendation of an investigatory board that American harbor fortifications be reinforced by constructing a class of "sea-going armored vessels."

THE NEW BATTLESHIP NAVY

Congressional investigators revealed the depths to which American naval power had sunk. Both major political parties then began to champion revitalization programs—each naturally blaming the other for the problems. Bipartisan and intersectional support eventually brought about naval rehabilitation.

The two "sea-going armored vessels" authorized in 1886 became the *Maine* and *Texas*. Both were of foreign design, and both were partially rigged for sails. Certain parts had to be imported. The armor was of oil-tempered steel, which was soon found to be weak. *Texas* mounted only two large guns; *Maine* had four

of moderate size. Both ships relied on the crude iron gun sights their predecessors had used during the Civil War. Neither ship had much range or speed. *Maine* proved to be highly vulnerable, and it is remembered principally for the fact that it blew up mysteriously in Havana harbor during 1898, precipitating the Spanish-American War.

Secretary of the Navy Benjamin F. Tracy presided over the resurgence of American naval power during the administration of President Benjamin Harrison. Tracy, a former Civil War general, befriended a bookish officer with a penchant for historical writing named Alfred Thayer Mahan. Captain Mahan's ideas concerning the importance of naval strength accorded with Tracy's, and the group of influential navalists with whom he associated. Congressional approval for battleship construction coincided with publication of Mahan's classic book, *The Influence of Sea Power Upon History* (1890)—and not by accident.

Mahan prophetically equated sea power with the nation's manifest destiny. According to the captain, American prosperity depended upon overseas commercial expansion, necessitating a powerful navy and foreign bases to protect and extend its benefits. A strong navy was the key to national power and security. Mahan articulated a theory of naval operations based on an offensive strategy designed to command the seas by concentrating powerful fleets against rivals in decisive engagements. Mahan derided the commerce raiding/coastal defense idea— the basic U.S. naval policy since the Revolution—and called instead for wide-ranging fleets of battleships to master the seas.

Mahan's ideas found immediate favor worldwide. Kaiser Wilhelm for instance, ordered his naval officers to read *The Influence of Sea Power*, and he distributed copies to all of Germany's libraries. Japanese naval officers memorized it— in English—as part of their intensive training. Mahan's numerous works were translated into French, Italian, and Russian. The English especially lionized Mahan since he outlined a policy they seemed already to have been following.

In the United States, Mahan contributed greatly to a naval renaissance by producing an intellectual synthesis relating sea power to American history and to successful diplomacy.

Tracy quoted Mahan in his annual reports to the Secretary of War and called for the construction of two fleets of battleships along with numerous auxiliary vessels. In June, 1890, Congress approved the construction of three "sea-going coastline battleships designed to carry the heaviest armor and the most powerful ordnance." The word "battleship" thus appeared for the first time in an official American state paper.

Indiana, *Oregon*, and *Massachusetts*, the first three American battleships, were heavily armed and well protected. The ships were slow. By world standards, they had a low freeboard (meaning the distance between the deck and the water level). But the appearance of battleships, their steady improvement, and their increasing numbers marked a shift in U.S. naval strategy towards the offensive Mahanian vision of naval forces. Within twenty years after authorizing its first battleship, the American Navy had a fleet of twenty-five. By 1903, naval authorities and politicians were calling for a fleet of forty-eight battleships.

The revitalization of the Navy helped forge close ties between representatives of industry and government. Meeting the Navy's demands for battleships and other vessels stimulated and particularly benefited the steel industry. Armor production, for example, including the factories themselves, arose in response to Navy contracts.

The science of armor production and its steady improvement helped encourage the continual modernization of steel plants. In 1880, for example, cast-iron plates fifteen inches thick represented the basic raw material of armor. Within a year, the same defensive quality was achieved by a twelve-inch thickness of "composite" armor—manufactured by facing wrought iron with steel. An American named Hayward Harvey developed a face-hardening technique in 1890 which allowed 7.5 inches of his nickel-treated steel to withstand the same punishment, and weigh much less, than 12 inches of wrought-iron composite armor. Five years later, the Krupp firm of Germany introduced a new variety of steel which increased the strength, but not the weight, of armor by another 30 per cent. American steel corporations such as Bethlehem and Carnegie soon acquired licenses to produce Krupp armor.

American battleships incorporated modern improvements in their construction. When Congress approved three new battleships in 1896, for instance, they directed that the recommendations proposed by an investigatory board be followed regarding the designs of the *Illinois*, *Alabama*, and *Wisconsin*. The design emphasized seagoing qualities like a high freeboard and good range.

State officials began taking an interest in the *Wisconsin* immediately. Governor William H. Upham appointed a commission of prominent citizens to carry out the official duties involving the ship. U.S. Senator Isaac Stephenson of Marinette headed the commission. The senator's daughter Elizabeth became *Wisconsin*'s sponsor. Milwaukee Road railway directors provided a special train for the commissioners to use on their excursion to San Francisco during November, 1898.

Some 1,500 citizens cheered when Elizabeth Stephenson broke two bottles of champagne against *Wisconsin*'s bow—one a bottle of French vintage carried across the continent and the other, of California vintage, supplied by shipyard workers. In his speech, Lt.-Governor Emil Baensch then made note of the state's own important shipbuilding industry which produced "powerful and progressive yet peaceful" vessels. Wisconsinites, he observed, "hailed with delight" the launching of their namesake battleship. U.S. Senator John L. Mitchell of Milwaukee hoped that the new battleship would never be compelled to fire its guns except in practice. "She will bear our name, but she will fly the American flag," Senator Mitchell concluded, advising world powers such as England to take notice of the growing naval strength of the United States.

The *Wisconsin*, like its sisters, had four heavy 13-inch main battery guns mounted in two innovative balanced turrets featuring sloped armored faces (rather than the pillbox style used since the days of *Monitor*), setting the style for subsequent battleships. Two modern three-cylinder triple-expansion steam engines generated 12,322 horsepower which could propel the ship at 16.5 knots. Electricity powered the turrets, ventilating fans, and ammunition hoists.

U.S.S. Wisconsin *(BB-9) under construction at the Union Iron Works, San Francisco, October, 1897. The Spanish-American War, which made the United States a world power, occurred while the* Wisconsin *was under construction.*

Harveyized nickel steel main-belt armor, tapering from 16.5 inches on top to 9.5 inches on the bottom and to not less than 4 inches on the bow, provided the basic waterline protection. Other armor covered much of the midship area, the gun positions, the conning tower, and the signal bridge. The *Wisconsin* had excellent and easily accessible coal storage and boiler room arrangements. Fourteen quick-firing 6-inch guns were mounted in hull and upper deck casemates, and four torpedo tubes could fire from broadside positions above the waterline. *Wisconsin* was a formidable man-of-war.

Union Iron Works of San Francisco built the *Wisconsin* for $4,162,617. She measured 373 feet long by 72 feet wide and weighed 11,564 tons, the largest warship built on the Pacific Coast. The Carnegie Steel Company supplied all 2,559 tons of armor for the ship. At full complement, *Wisconsin* held thirty-five officers and 496 men of other ranks.

Acceptance trials in 1900 demonstrated *Wisconsin*'s qualities. Chief Engineer J. K. Robin-son observed "throughout the trial all the machinery worked with the greatest of regularity and smoothness." The "exceptionally successful trial" showed the *Wisconsin* to be an "easy steamer" and "an excellent gun platform." Like its two sister ships, the *Wisconsin* represented a genuine advance in American naval armament.

Union Iron Works employees were building the *Wisconsin* when the Spanish-American War occurred, but her career was profoundly influenced by the outcome of the conflict because it left Americans with overseas colonies and protectorates to care for. American interests in the Caribbean and in the distant Pacific became more focused as a result of the war.

The Spanish-American War also vindicated the concentrated fleet action theory of Captain Mahan. America's stunning naval victories in Cuba and at Manila Bay seemed to prove that modern fleets were indeed worth their cost. More battleships would be needed, some argued, to defend the new empire that the new Navy had made possible.

BATTLESHIP DIPLOMACY

THE *Wisconsin* spent her early years operating from West Coast ports, symbolizing the importance which American attached to the Pacific. President Theodore Roosevelt, himself a naval historian and an enthusiastic supporter of Captain Mahan and his battleship-centered ideas, energetically promoted naval building programs. The United States built sixteen new battleships and rose to become a recognized world power during the seven years of his presidency. In 1907, Roosevelt sent the entire American battleship fleet on an epic and unprecedented world cruise which drew international attention to American strength.

Wisconsin state officials accompanied President Roosevelt on his trip to California in May, 1901. Julius Bleyer, editor of the Milwaukee *Evening Wisconsin*, headed the official commission to formally present the new battleship *Wisconsin* with its state-donated silver service. The *Wisconsin* departed from San Francisco immediately thereafter, assured that citizens from the Badger State would take a continued interest in her career.

The *Wisconsin* visited Hawaii that fall in company with *Oregon* and *Iowa*. At the end of 1901 *Wisconsin* traveled to Samoa, hosting the German provincial governor. German-American tension had centered on Samoa some years before until both agreed to share privileges there.

U.S.S. Wisconsin *in San Francisco bay, 1901, at a review in honor of President Theodore Roosevelt. The ship's "fighting tops" and hull-mounted gun sponsons were leftovers from the age of sail.*

U.S. Naval Historical Center

Battleships of the Great White Fleet steaming out of Hampton Roads, Virginia, December, 1907, on the first leg of their fifteen-month world cruise.

Wisconsin became flagship of the Pacific Squadron in 1902, and the presidents of Peru and Chile came aboard the ship when it visited South America.

American interest in various inter-oceanic canal projects focused diplomatic attention on the domestic affairs of the Colombian province of Panama during 1902. Some Panamanians wanted their independence from Colombia and civil discontent had erupted into violent disorder. The *Wisconsin* anchored off the west coast of Panama one breezy October day in order to provide a meeting site for Colombian, Panamanian, and U.S. diplomats. After negotiating for a month, the parties arranged a truce which became known as "The Peace of *Wisconsin*."

Panama became an independent nation in the fall of 1903, and its leaders quickly agreed to permit the United States to build a ship canal linking the Atlantic and Pacific oceans. President Roosevelt listed the treaty authorizing American control of the Panama Canal as one of his administration's two most important foreign affairs accomplishments. The other achievement, Roosevelt believed, was the 46,000-mile world cruise of the U.S. battleship fleet.

President Roosevelt ordered the most powerful group of warships ever assembled in the Western Hemisphere to collect at Hampton Roads, Virginia, in December, 1907. Sixteen battleships and numerous lesser craft took on supplies in preparation for a trip around Cape Horn to visit the West Coast. The fleet's 14,000 sailors loaded 35 million pounds of explosive projectiles; 6 million pounds of meat, fruit, cereal, and vegetables; 15,000 pounds of plum pudding; 15,000 pounds of candy; fifty phonographs; 400 sheets of "the latest popular songs"; 300 chess sets; and the first portion of the 435,000 tons of coal eventually consumed on the fifteen-month voyage. Rear Admiral R. D. Evans, Fleet Commander, noted that his men "were ready for a fight or a frolic," and since President Roosevelt had kept the purpose and ultimate extent of the voyage a secret, Admiral Evans' description was an apt one.

Friendly demonstrators greeted the U.S. sailors along their route at ports in Brazil, Argentina, Chile, and Peru, but the frenzied rejoicing that gripped residents of California exceeded all expectations. Californians cheered lustily when Admiral Evans stated that, in his opinion, the United States needed "more battleships and fewer statesmen."

The *Wisconsin* joined the fleet at San Francisco. Its hull inspected and pronounced "excellent," Captain Henry Morrell made ready

18

for his ship's longest cruise. President Roosevelt wanted to demonstrate American strength in the western Pacific to one of America's international rivals, the Japanese.

The battleships—popularly known as the Great White Fleet because of the heat-reflecting white paint they wore to reduce interior temperatures—set out across the Pacific. Celebrations marked their arrival in Honolulu, Auckland, Sydney, and Melbourne. When the battleships of the Great White Fleet arrived at Yokohama they found the Japanese battle fleet had put to sea—its location unknown. The Japanese public, however, seemed as warmly hospitable as the citizens of other nations. Great fun, apparently, was had by all, and subtle tensions between the two new Pacific naval powers subsided.

The fleet then visited China before heading to Manila where preparations were made to cross the Indian Ocean via Ceylon. From there, the fleet transited the Suez Canal and moved westward through the Mediterranean. The battleships then steamed across the Atlantic to arrive at Hampton Roads on Washington's Birthday, where President Roosevelt reviewed them.

The *Wisconsin* participated in the various fleet maneuvers while underway. On an average pleasant day the ship's engines consumed seventy to eighty tons of coal and 6,000 gallons of fresh water. A speed of 10.5 knots required a comfortable 72 rpm from the propellers and drove the ship about 250 miles in twenty-four hours.

The battleship's crew had numerous responsibilities. The hierarchy of rank represented only part of *Wisconsin*'s division of labor, for every man also had a specialized skill. Work was carried out by dividing the crew into functional units and simultaneously assigning and scheduling duties according to each man's place aboard ship and by time. Thus, *Wisconsin* crewmen were attached to either the port or starboard watch and were assigned duties as members of one of seven divisions—gunnery, engineering, marines, etc. Most activities required units smaller in size than watches or divisions, so crewmen were further assigned to station bills, quarter watches, and to individual numbers. Each crewman ate, slept, and stored his gear in a particular spot. Daily schedules specified when certain tasks would be carried out. Such shipboard duties as sanding the deck with holystones, chipping and painting, polishing the brightwork, preparing food, cleaning, refueling, and standing watches were highly routinized.

Crew members slept in hammocks. Crowded berthing spaces necessitated superimposing the hammocks, making entrance and exit to one's suspended sleeping quarters difficult. "You could sleep only if you were very tired," recalled one *Wisconsin* veteran, and falling out of one's hammock commonly identified inexperienced sailors.

Sailors of the Great White Fleet ate in separate groups of about twenty-five men called "messes." Each mess had its own equipment, table, and cook. Food varied. Eggs, coffee, po-

Jolly tars posed on the foredeck of the Wisconsin, *c. 1901.*

SHSW WHi(X3)36911

H.M.S. Dreadnought, *launched in 1906, revolutionized battleship construction. She was fast and heavily armed, with ten 12-inch guns in five turrets.*

tatoes, corn beef, pork chops, apple sauce, tea, butter, and bread were regularly available along with hardtack crackers. Fresh fruits and vegetables could be obtained at most ports, and American battleships had refrigeration units to reduce spoilage. Indeed, living conditions aboard American battleships were much better than those of other nations. Sailor life at the turn of the century was not especially burdensome, and it was often pleasant. Seafaring offered the lure of travel, adventure, camaraderie, and excitement.

The quality of enlisted personnel rose along with the New Navy itself. The Navy sought to attract the manpower of small-town mid-America after 1890, establishing recruiting centers in Great Lakes communities like Chicago, Detroit, Duluth, and Milwaukee as well as in landlocked states such as Kansas, Nebraska, and Colorado. By 1900, over 85 per cent of America's sailors were citizens—by contrast with the Navy of the Civil War era. Training and educational programs had begun to transform enlisted men from the ignorant maritime laborers of the age of sail into nautical technicians.

The voyage of the Great White Fleet was a genuine technical achievement. The professional skills displayed by the American fleet astonished foreign naval authorities. The cruise experience, moreover, provided lessons in high seas sailing, planning of subsistence and living quarters, ventilation and sanitation requirements, and many features of ship design. The world cruise also proved that the American fleet could operate at great distances from home, a demonstration of its long-range mobility. The U.S. had became a world power, and, as President Roosevelt explained, "nobody after this will forget that the American coast is on the Pacific as well as the Atlantic."

When the sailors of the Great White Fleet returned to the United States early in 1909, they discovered that the British had commissioned a vastly improved battleship—H.M.S. *Dreadnought.* The battleships of the Great White Fleet were suddenly antiquated by comparison. The *Dreadnought* mounted so many more heavy guns, possessed such thick armor, and had such great speed that it represented a quantum leap forward in naval armament. Thereafter, battleships constructed to its pattern would be known as dreadnoughts, while those built prior to its appearance were classified as predreadnoughts.

The voyage of the Great White Fleet and the appearance of the *Dreadnought* contributed to a surging worldwide interest in battleships. "Battleship mania" gripped nations as they sought new capital ships. Denmark, Spain, Sweden, and the Netherlands acquired their first battleships; France, Italy, Russia, and Japan increased the numbers of battleships they were constructing; Siam, Greece, Turkey, Argentina, Brazil, Chile, and Portugal began purchasing battleships. American diplomats avidly promoted the sale of American-built battleships in South America. England and Germany, meanwhile, accelerated their battleship-centered naval arms race.

THE GREAT WAR

THE years before World War I were marked by frenzied battleship construction. The United States, for example, possessed twenty-five pre-dreadnought battleships in 1914, and had built or was building fourteen additional dreadnoughts. The U.S. Navy ranked third in the world, behind England and Germany.

American ships adopted centralized fire-control equipment which increased accurate gunnery ranges first to 10,000 yards and by 1917 to 16,000 yards (eight nautical miles). American dreadnought battleships like the *Nevada, Oklahoma, Arizona,* and *Pennsylvania* pioneered new concepts in armor protection. An "all or nothing" rationale reduced the extent of armored areas on U.S. battleships in favor of carrying the thickest possible armor to protect its vital machinery, buoyancy, and fighting ability. An armored box protected the midships area, covering propulsion equipment and magazines. The conning tower command center was armored, together with main battery gun turrets and associated systems. Two armored decks afforded protection from the "plunging" fire of shells fired at long range. This armor scheme became known as "raft-body armor," and American ship design became recognized as among the best in the world.

President Woodrow Wilson hoped to avoid becoming involved in the European war which erupted in 1914. He supported military preparedness to help maintain American neutral-

Splendid view of crew, foredeck, and bridge of U.S.S. Wisconsin, *flagship of the Pacific Squadron, 1903. Her main armament consisted of four 13-inch guns.*

1903 USS Wisconsin Cruise Book

U.S.S. Wisconsin *(BB-9) in the Gatun Locks, Panama Canal, July, 1915. Note the distinctive "cage" masts, outfitted in 1909 to afford the ship's gunners better fire control.*

ity. The policy of preparedness included a large program of naval armaments. Navy Secretary Josephus Daniels called for the U.S. Navy to be "second to none" in 1916, and President Wilson approved the largest warship-building program in American history. The 1916 Naval Act authorized the construction of ten battleships which, if completed within the three-year plan, would have left the United States with thirty-five improved oil-burning dreadnoughts, or slightly more than Great Britain.

American participation in World War I decisively aided England and France. But ironically, its entry into the war pointed out America's lack of a properly balanced fleet. Battleships seemed unnecessary once the Royal Navy had confined Germany's capital ships to their ports. Smaller warships, however, to escort the convoys of American troops and supply ships and to screen them from enemy submarines, were in short supply.

Old battleships, some from the Great White Fleet era, came back into service during 1914–1918. The *Wisconsin*, for instance, was recom-missioned in 1915 to serve as a training ship. She patrolled the coastal waters between Virginia and New York during the war, becoming a school ship for firemen, engineers, signalmen, and steersmen. Secretary Daniels reviewed the *Wisconsin* in New York Harbor in late 1918. After that, the battleship headed to the Caribbean for its final cruise season before returning to Philadelphia, where it remained inactive until decommissioning in May, 1920.

THE TREATY SYSTEM

KEY elements of American foreign policy merged with naval affairs after the war. The U.S. concept of a "navy second to none," for example, challenged England's traditional policy of naval supremacy in the Atlantic and upset Japan's view of its own pre-eminence in the western Pacific. The United States, England, and Japan therefore began a competitive round of battleship construction immediately following the war's end. The naval race met with widespread public disapproval, however, and American diplomats called for an international conference on arms reduction to take place in Washington during late 1921.

The Washington Treaty (1922) and subsequent naval agreements restricted battleship numbers as well as their weight and armament. England, France, Italy, Japan, and the United States agreed to limit battleship construction. Older battleships, like the *Wisconsin*, were scrapped.* A quota assigned a proportional battleship strength ratio to each power. Battleships could not exceed 35,000 tons displacement nor mount guns greater than 16-inch. The agreement permitted the United States to complete the *Colorado* and *West Virginia* for a total of eighteen battleships.

The treaty system profoundly effected battleship development. The displacement restrictions, for instance, encouraged the introduction of weight-saving techniques. Oil-powered, geared, high-pressure steam turbine engines generated both weight savings and tremendous horsepower gains. Treaty-approved reconstruction programs allowed substantial improvements to be made to existing battleships. Thus upgraded, battleships became even more prized since their numbers remained constant.

At the same time, certain visionaries began questioning the value of battleships. Aircraft and submarines (and the torpedoes they carried) seemed to make battleships vulnerable and obsolete. Air power advocates such as General Billy Mitchell insisted that planes would replace navies. Indeed, Mitchell demonstrated that bomb-carrying aircraft could sink an old battleship at anchor.

Naval authorities, meanwhile, carried out extensive weapons tests of their own, using ships scrapped by the Washington Treaty as targets. The tests showed how difficult it was to hit, let alone sink, moving battleships with bombs or torpedoes. Naval architects suggested that thick armored decks, greater speed, ship-mounted antiaircraft guns, and improved underwater compartmentalization would prevent bombs or torpedoes from sinking battleships. The tests also showed heavy guns to be the most effective naval weapons by far. Aircraft and submarines

obviously increased the dangers which battleships might face in future wars, but naval planners concluded that the new weapons did not render battleships obsolete. To reduce the threat of air attack, battleships could be accompanied by recently introduced aircraft carriers whose planes could form a protective "air umbrella" over the vessels. Thus, in the minds of naval and political leaders, the battleship remained the primary unit for calculating maritime strength in the postwar period.

THE FAST BATTLESHIPS

THE treaty system broke down during the 1930's. France and Italy began building new battleships in 1931. Japan announced its intention to withdraw from the treaty system in 1934. Nazi Germany and Soviet Russia had not been parties to the naval limitation agreements, and they too began working on modern battleships. Both England and the United States followed suit.

A new generation of battleships emerged. The introduction of lightweight alloys, very high-powered engines, and innovative defense systems—all stimulated by treaty system restrictions—produced radically improved battleship designs. Naval architects throughout the world designed faster, bigger, more stable, better armed, and more costly battleships.

President Franklin D. Roosevelt took great interest in naval matters. A thoroughgoing student of Mahan and a one-time Assistant Secretary of the Navy, Roosevelt favored the Navy over the other military services. (During meetings with representatives of the Navy and the Army, for instance, he referred to Navy officials as "us" and to Army officers as "them.") When Roosevelt called upon the United States to build a "two-ocean Navy," he had already secured congressional approval for ten new battleships.

The United States began building battleships in 1938 after a hiatus of nearly two decades. When launched in 1940, the *North Carolina* marked the emergence of a different sort of capital ship—the fast battleship. It embodied modern characteristics. The quest for speed necessitated a long, fine hull shape in addition to tremendous horsepower. Radar, for example, though still primitive, and vastly improved

* The Hitner Salvage Corporation of Philadelphia purchased the *Wisconsin* from the Navy for $41,812.50. The ship was dismantled and broken up for scrap after delivery to the purchaser on April 24, 1922.

fire-control apparatus enabled the ship's 16-inch guns to shoot up to 35,000 yards accurately—nearly twenty miles. Spotter aircraft launched from the ship helped direct its gunfire. The United States began constructing a second group of fast battleships in 1939, followed by yet another group in 1940.

The final group of four fast battleships became known as the *Iowa* class. Without question, they were the best ever built. They possessed an unequalled combination of great offensive power, good armor and antiaircraft protection, and very high speed. No other battleships matched the *Iowa, New Jersey, Missouri,* and *Wisconsin.*

Serious work on the *Iowa*s began after secret information concerning new Japanese battleship construction became available to Navy planners in 1937. Captain Allan J. Chantry was largely responsible for the design of the *Iowa*-class battleships, and President Roosevelt supported his work wholeheartedly. Chantry's design emphasized a compact superstructure and

Close-up of BB-64's conning tower command area, showing the massive door and 17-inch armor.

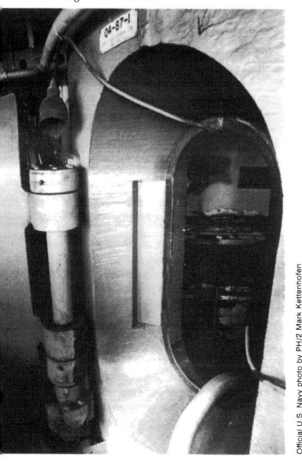

long, graceful lines, coupled with extremely powerful engines. His design was reminiscent of an exotic sports car eighteen stories high.

Chantry submitted his plans in June, 1938. They called for ships 880 feet in length, 108 feet in width (narrow enough to pass through the Panama Canal with two feet to spare), capable of achieving speeds of thirty-three knots per hour with 212,000-horsepower engines, drawing no more than thirty-six feet of water, and possessing a very long range. Chantry's plan recommended that the ships mount nine improved 16-inch guns in three turrets (two forward and one aft).

The 16-inch, 50-caliber gun was the most destructive cannon ever mounted on an American ship. At forty-five degrees of elevation it could fire either a 2,700-pound armor-piercing or a 1,900-pound explosive bombardment projectile some twenty-four miles. Each gun weighed 240,000 pounds and was nearly sixty-eight feet long; each could fire two rounds per minute. The armor-piercing projectile was propelled by a 660-pound charge of powder. The bombardment shell used half that charge.

Captain Chantry also planned the defenses of the *Iowa*s. A 464-foot-long armored box 12.2 inches thick surrounded the ship's vitals. Horizontal protection was achieved by three armored decks. The main protective deck (about 6 inches in thickness) was reinforced above by a bomb deck which added 1.25 inches of armor, and by a splinter deck below which added yet another half-inch of armor. A partial third armored deck 6 inches thick ran for 100 feet from behind the number three turret to the after end of the steering gear. Armor of up to 17.5 inches thick protected parts of the turrets, the barbettes, and the conning tower command area. Triple bottoms and minute underwater compartmentalization protected the ship's hull from the effects of torpedoes. Armored transverse bulkheads 14 inches thick helped ensure buoyancy for the hull's main body. In all, slightly over 10,000 tons of armor protected the ship. Twenty 5-inch, 38-caliber dual-purpose guns and, ultimately, sixty-five light antiaircraft weapons bristled from the decks.

Chantry's impressive, ultra-fast battleship design received considerable attention from Navy war planners. Since the *Iowa*s would be

These 16-inch projectiles for the Wisconsin's *main battery weigh between 1,900 and 2,700 pounds each. They can be hurled up to twenty-four miles—about the distance from downtown Milwaukee to Port Washington in Ozaukee County.*

faster than all other fast battleships, their operational missions might be different from those of other battleships. Rather than merely buttress the fleet battle line (which they certainly could do), the *Iowa*s might also be used for detached or "eccentric operations." Their phenomenal speed and destroyer-like maneuverability, together with great endurance, would enable them to pursue fast-moving Japanese cruisers, for example; to seek and destroy heavy surface commerce raiders, such as the ones Nazi Germany had built; or, in conjunction with other U.S. ships, to form a "striking force" to raid enemy commerce. On the eve of World War II, strategic planners envisioned naval task groups composed of several *Iowa*s, escorted by supporting aircraft carriers and destroyers, operating deep in the Pacific.

WORLD WAR II

THE outbreak of war in 1939 stimulated American military construction. Germany's rapid conquest of France electrified American war planners, while Japan's aggressiveness in the Pacific led to steadily deteriorating relations between the United States and the Imperial government.

At dawn on December 7, 1941, Japanese carrier planes carried out a surprise attack against the battleships of the U.S. Pacific Fleet anchored at Pearl Harbor in Hawaii. Japanese airmen devastated them in a stunning blow, sinking the *Arizona*, *West Virginia*, *Oklahoma*, *Nevada*, and *California*; damaging the *Maryland*, *Tennessee*, and *Pennsylvania*.* What President Roosevelt described as a "day of infamy" brought an angry and united America into World War II.

The Japanese had clearly demonstrated the ability of aircraft to sink operational battleships. (Three days later, Japanese planes sank two powerful British warships, the *Repulse* and *Prince of Wales*, off the coast of Malaya.) Pearl Harbor did not put an immediate end to the battleship building programs then underway

*All but the *Arizona* and *Oklahoma* were salvaged and repaired for service in the war.

25

U.S.S. Wisconsin *(BB-64) under construction in the Philadelphia Navy Yard, January, 1943. The streamlined hull, 887 feet long and 108 feet wide, helped make the* Iowa-*class battleships the sleekest and fastest warships of World War II.*

throughout the world, however, and battleships continued to play a role in the naval campaigns of World War II. But they were not used in the manner which Captain Mahan and all world naval powers had envisioned they would be. There were no general fleet engagements of battleships fought to command the seas. Instead, aircraft carriers, once believed to be subsidiary escorts for battleships, now became capital ships. Carriers effectively assumed the decisive role traditionally reserved for battleships because they could launch their aircraft hundreds of miles away from their targets. Indeed, the decisive engagement of the war in the Pacific—Midway—was fought entirely by aircraft launched from ships which never saw each other.

The greatest naval expansion in world history took place between 1941 and 1945. The U.S. Navy mushroomed from a force of 160,997 men operating 1,099 vessels to 3,383,196 men and 50,759 vessels. The 43,000-member work force of the Philadelphia Naval Shipyard alone, for instance, produced 1,300 vessels during the war, including several aircraft carriers and the *Iowa*-class battleships *New Jersey* and *Wisconsin*.

Seven thousand workers were assigned to begin *Wisconsin* in January, 1941, after President Roosevelt developed what he described as a "simple rule" for naming the vessel. By selecting state names for the new ships from the list of old battleships stricken from the Navy's inventory, the President believed he would "avoid any heart burnings by proponents of other states."

State citizens took an immediate interest in the *Wisconsin*. Governor Walter S. Goodland's wife Madge became the battleship's sponsor. Roosevelt's Chief of Staff, Fleet Admiral William D. Leahy, a native of Ashland, brought the old battleship *Wisconsin*'s state-donated silver service to Madison when he addressed the legislature. Members of the governor's commission appointed to carry out official duties regarding the new ship placed the silver on display in the capitol as their contribution "to the naval enlistments from our state." Schoolchildren and others volunteered to christen the new battleship, some recommending that Wisconsin River water be used instead of champagne.

Building the *Wisconsin* consumed two lives and 2,891,334 man-days. It cost over $110 million and was completed in a record-breaking thirty-nine months. The complex battleship required thousands of separate working plans. There were 700 plans for ordnance, 6,000 hull plans, 2,400 electrical plans, and 2,700 plans for its machinery—all of which consumed 348,000 pounds of blueprint paper. Workmen installed 2,990 telephones, 5,000 lighting fixtures, 14,000 valves for *Wisconsin*'s forty-two miles of piping, and a generating system that could electrify the city of Seattle. The *Wisconsin* consumed over 1,000,000 rivets, 4,300,000 feet of welding rods, and 312,000 pounds of paint.

Parts for the *Wisconsin* came from around the nation, and sometimes delays occurred. One of the ship's two 200,000-pound rudder posts, for instance, was held up when the river barge carrying it to Philadelphia became trapped by winter's ice.

Workers installed the turrets after the ship's hull had been launched. Each of *Wisconsin*'s complicated turret mechanisms weighed over 3,000,000 pounds without the guns, or about the same as a destroyer. Built on shore and then dismantled one section at a time for reassembly aboard ship, the 350-ton pieces were carefully fitted in place, using special micrometer gauges to ensure accuracy of levels and centers.

Some 100,000 pounds of grease helped ease the *Wisconsin* down the ways and into the Delaware River on December 7, 1943. Madge Goodland christened the immense polished hull with a bottle of champagne. Under Secretary of the Navy Ralph A. Bard delivered the main address. He explained that *Wisconsin* represented an "instrument of retaliation" against Japan for its sneak attack on Pearl Harbor. He went on to extol the virtues of the Badger State, its shipbuilding industry, its fishing and hunting resources, and its numerous tourist attractions.

Some 1,500 people attended *Wisconsin*'s commissioning ceremony at Philadelphia in April, 1944. Senator Robert M. La Follette, Jr., and three members of the state's congressional delegation were present. Mrs. Carl Pick of West Bend presented a plaque to the ship that had been cast at her husband's foundry from metal

U.S. Naval Historical Center

The Wisconsin *moored alongside the hulk of the battleship* Oklahoma, *Pearl Harbor, November, 1944. The* Iowa-*class ship dwarfs the older vessel, which was sunk by the Japanese on December 7, 1941, and subsequently raised for salvage.*

salvaged from the first battleship *Wisconsin's* whistle. Ten other veterans of the first U.S.S. *Wisconsin* were present, including the new ship's commander, Captain Earl E. Stone.

Born in Milwaukee in 1895, Stone had attended the city's public schools and its state university before being appointed to the U.S. Naval Academy with the help of the elder Senator La Follette. Stone trained aboard the old *Wisconsin* during its midshipman's cruise of 1916. He became a radio officer after World War I, serving on cruisers and destroyers. Stone took engineering courses, and in 1925 he graduated from Harvard University with a Master of Science degree. Administrative jobs in Washington followed. When Japanese planes sank the U.S.S. *California* at Pearl Harbor, Stone was the ship's executive officer.

Stone delivered the main address at *Wisconsin's* commissioning ceremony. He spoke about the power of modern battleships and their ability to protect themselves from airplanes. He predicted that *Wisconsin's* role in the war would be to add its weight to the all-out struggle then in progress. Finally he expressed his feeling of "great pride and responsibility" to be in command of the ship named for his own home state.

The new battleship and its mostly inexperienced crew set out to the Caribbean for a shakedown cruise between May and August of 1944. Final adjustments were made during September at Philadelphia when *Wisconsin* became fully operational. The great ship transited the Panama Canal on its way to the Pacific, joining the Third Fleet at Ulithi Atoll in the Caroline Islands.

Wisconsin, like the others *Iowa*s, was designed in 1938 for a crew of just under 2,000. But the addition of numerous antiaircraft weapons, radar, and increasingly sophisticated electronics gear necessitated larger crews by 1944. *Wisconsin* put to sea with 2,724 crewmen in fourteen divisions. "Every inch of space was utilized," recalled Gunners Mate Third Class Richard D. Friend of Fort Wayne, Indiana.

Overcrowding occurred. Extra four-tiered metal bunks were installed. "It took a little maneuvering" to get into one's bunk, recalled a *Wisconsin* veteran, and "there was only enough room to sleep." Seamen could not sit up in their bunks. Thin mattresses fitted over canvas slings provided modest comfort at best, and the ship's 84,480 feet of ventilating ducts carried no air-conditioning. Interior temperatures became uncomfortably warm in topical climates. Some crewmen slept on the teak deck under the stars where it was cooler, recalled Seaman First Class Herbert F. Laufenburg of Milwaukee. Officers' quarters were likewise spartan and overpopulated.

Enlisted men ate in a single cafeteria-style mess. Food quality was good; the cooking, however, varied. On long and dangerous deployments, such as the *Wisconsin* undertook during the late spring of 1945, fresh fruits and vegetables could not be obtained for a month. For the most part, however, *Wisconsin* was well-provisioned, and the availability of good food contributed to the crew's high morale. The provisioning of a battleship was nothing less than awesome. Each day of World War II—with one month's exception—*Wisconsin* crewmen consumed on average 4,110 pounds of vegetables, 1,640 pounds of fruit, 1,500 pounds of flour, 2,465 pounds of meat, 164 pounds of butter, 540 dozen eggs, 820 candy bars, 875 quarts of ice cream, 205 pounds of coffee, and 275 bars of soap.

The morale and spirit of *Wisconsin*'s crew were "fantastic," according to Fire Controlman Second Class Roland Steinle, Jr., of Milwaukee. Captain Stone, a reflective, soft-spoken man, made an effort to get to know his crew. Naval discipline remained firm, but Stone did "quite a bit" for morale-building purposes. Movies were shown frequently, mail service received special attention, liberty parties went ashore whenever practical, officers ensured that

Wisconsin remained spotless, and the men kept their uniforms and equipment immaculately clean. *Wisconsin* sported a band, a newsletter, and an excellent boxing team.

The various rites of passage long celebrated by sailors remained features of battleship life. Hazing and other forms of initiation marked the transformation of "pollywogs" into "shellbacks" at the court of King Neptune after crossing the Equator. These ceremonies served to temporarily relax the minutely organized and routinized life of deployed sailors. The *Wisconsin* had a reputation as being a "happy ship." "I enjoyed being on it," recalled Boatswain's Mate Second Class John Rymenams of Racine.

During the war battleships gave antiaircraft protection to carriers, shelled enemy shore installations, covered amphibious assaults, and refueled destroyers. Their sick bays and medical staffs provided aid for the wounded; their seaplanes rescued downed pilots. They even took part in a few surface engagements. Battleships did everything, in short, except what they had been designed to do: namely, to engage fleets of enemy battleships. The *Wisconsin* took part in every campaign undertaken in the

Turret crew loading 110-pound bags of powder for Wisconsin's *16-inch guns during the Okinawa campaign, May, 1945.*

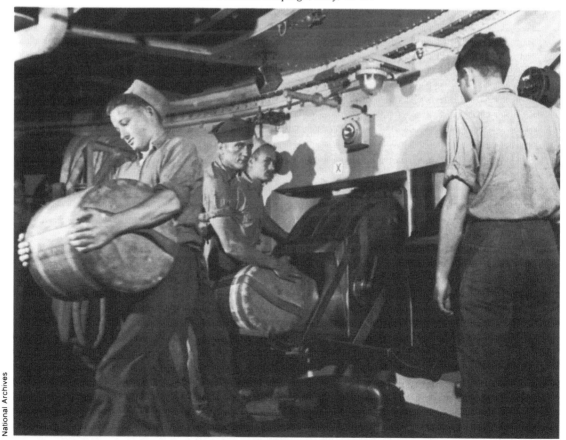

Wisconsin on maneuvers off Hampton Roads, Virginia, in the 1950's. Note the ship's clean lines and compact superstructure. At speed, the Iowa-class battleship has a tighter turning radius than a destroyer.

Pacific Theater from the moment it arrived in the war zone until Japan surrendered nine months later.

Wisconsin became part of Fast Carrier Task Force 38 in December, 1944, just after the naval battle of Leyte Gulf. Admiral William Halsey's Third Fleet covered the troop landings on Mindoro and Luzon in the Philippine Islands, and the carrier task force launched attacks against Japanese shore facilities. A great typhoon struck Halsey's fleet on December 17, sinking three American destroyers while sweeping one of *Wisconsin*'s Kingfisher aircraft off the port catapult and damaging two others.

The new year found *Wisconsin* supporting the Third Fleet's carrier operations. Carrier planes hit Japanese targets on northern Luzon and Formosa. The task group sortied into the South China Sea during mid-January, striking Saigon, Camranh Bay, Hong Kong, Canton, Hainan, and Okinawa. *Wisconsin* antiaircraft gunners opened fire on a Japanese observation plane on January 20 off the China coast, but scored no hits. Captain Stone's Action Report noted that crew and equipment had put forth "uniformly excellent performance." *Wisconsin*'s floatplanes attempted to rescue a downed American pilot, but could not locate the survivor.

Admiral Halsey transferred command in

February, 1945, and the ships of his Third Fleet became the Fifth Fleet. *Wisconsin* joined carrier task unit 58.2 as the flagship of Rear Admiral E. W. Hanson, moving northward to strike the Japanese home islands. Carrier planes blasted targets in the Tokyo area for two days without letup before retiring to cover landing operations on Iwo Jima. *Wisconsin*'s antiaircraft gunners drove off three Japanese planes attacking American shipping.

Wisconsin remained at Ulithi during early March. Captain Stone received a promotion and became a member of Pacific Fleet Commander Admiral Chester W. Nimitz's staff. Captain John W. Roper took command when Stone departed. Roper, an outspoken and powerful figure, drilled *Wisconsin*'s crew at Ulithi, particularly the antiaircraft gunners. Nevertheless, on March 11 three Japanese aircraft flying at wavetop level surprised the moored battleship at 8 P.M. and bombed the carrier *Randolph* in the adjacent berth where its crew had been watching a movie.

Fifth Fleet carriers stood out of Ulithi three days later, bound for southern Japan. The task force's mission was to cover the Okinawa landings. It turned out to be a ferocious four-month

air-sea battle. Military censors prevented the American public from knowing the full costs of the operation. Dozens of ships were damaged or sunk, and 5,000 American sailors died.

The Japanese had introduced bomb-loaded suicide plane attacks against American ships at Leyte Gulf in late 1944. Small numbers of suicide planes reappeared during the Iwo Jima campaign. Then the hopelessness of the military situation in mid-1945 caused Japan's leaders to unleash a desperate large-scale suicide plane campaign during the Okinawa operation. Against the crushing weight and overwhelming numbers of American forces assigned to capture the island, Japan committed its "divine wind" or kamikaze. Never in history would so much ammunition be flung into the air as during the battle for Okinawa.

While escorting the carriers off Kyushu, Japan, on a clear, calm day in mid-March, *Wisconsin*'s guns fired thousands of rounds at attacking Japanese planes. "Our gunfire made the sky look black," recalled a veteran. A Japanese aircraft broke through the American task force's air patrol at dawn, hitting the carrier *Enterprise* with a bomb after flying between the guns of *Wisconsin* and the destroyer *Langley*.

Wisconsin *taking evasive action during air attack off Okinawa, April, 1945. In the background, a U.S. fleet carrier has just taken a kamikaze hit.*

Wisconsin *under Japanese air attack off Okinawa, April 29, 1945.*

Wisconsin's forward antiaircraft control officer directed fire at a twin-engine bomber sweeping in towards the ship a half hour later. "He's coming right at us!" the officer screamed to 5-inch gun director Electronics Mate Second Class John Nazier of suburban Akron. Nazier prepared himself for a crash until he heard on his headset, "We've shot it down!" The bomber crashed 500 yards off *Wisconsin*'s starboard bow. Within minutes, *Wisconsin*'s guns hit another twin-engine bomber which fell close to the carrier *Intrepid*. A single-engine torpedo bomber swept in under the radar and out of the sun at 1 P.M., approaching the battleship on the port side. Gunners Mate Third Class John E. Champa, Jr., of West Allis directed the fire of six 20mm antiaircraft guns at the oncoming Japanese plane, and two pairs of heavier 40mm guns joined Champa. Champa recalled watching as the tracers of his weapon struck the airplane's wing, and how the bomber exploded before hitting the water. *Wisconsin* received credit for three Japanese planes and two assists that day.

A kamikaze hit the carrier *Franklin* the next morning. As the task force retired southward protecting the badly stricken carrier, *Wisconsin* gun crews claimed another Japanese plane.

One-third of *Wisconsin*'s crew maintained battle stations around the clock. General Quarters sounded before sunrise as scanners nervously watched the sky for approaching aircraft. On March 23 the *Wisconsin*, along with other ships, mistakenly fired on two American planes, shooting one down. Task force gunfire destroyed forty-eight Japanese planes during this phase of the Okinawa campaign.

The battleships *New Jersey*, *Missouri*, and *Wisconsin* bombarded the southeastern coast of Okinawa at the end of March, firing their 16-inch guns for five hours. It was *Wisconsin*'s first wartime bombardment, and gun trainer John Rymenams, stationed in turret number one, felt scared in his cramped armored quarters. Seventy-seven men worked each turret, thirty in the gun house alone. The lack of room magnified the sounds of turret and gun-operating machinery. The report of the 16-inch guns sounded "muffled," "hollow," "very low," and "not deafening." But the concussive forces unleashed by 16-inch gunfire generated enormous blast pressures. Rymenams felt these pressures right through armor when the guns of number two turret were fired. Electronics equipment was often damaged by blast pressures. Antiaircraft gunner Champa remembers that it was "very frightening" to be stationed on deck, as he was, when the 16-inch guns were firing. (The shelling so unnerved one *Wisconsin* seaman that he jumped overboard during the Okinawa bombardment and had to be rescued by destroyers.)

The carrier task force fended off Japanese air and naval attacks on American ground forces. Some 350 American carrier planes sank the giant Japanese battleship *Yamato* in early April when it attempted to attack the American ships around Okinawa, although a kamikaze struck and seriously damaged the carrier *Hancock* in return.

Fanatical kamikazes swarmed over the Americans in waves. The *Wisconsin*'s gunners fired at a kamikaze attacking *Missouri* from the stern in the late afternoon of April 11. Captain Roper's Action Report noted that the single-engine plane was "hit by *Wisconsin* gunfire but not effectively enough to deflect its run." The plane then struck *Missouri* on its starboard and

"careened in flames forward on her main deck." The exploding kamikaze caused little damage to the armored battleship. Another Japanese plane attacked *Wisconsin* from a similar position and was shot down within minutes, crashing 800 yards off the starboard quarter.

Suicide pilots carried out a series of daring air attacks against American ships near Okinawa four days later, and carrier *Intrepid* was struck in one such raid. *Wisconsin* crewmen watched as carrier *Bunker Hill* took two kamikaze hits several weeks later. Carrier *Enterprise* was damaged on May 15. A *Wisconsin* floatplane pilot rescued a downed aviator from carrier *Shangri-La* just before the Okinawa campaign ended. The Okinawa battles cost the Japanese 2,336 airplanes and left the pathway to Japan open.

After resting for three weeks in Leyte Gulf, the Fifth Fleet came under the command of Admiral Halsey and changed its name to the Third Fleet. Halsey planned to use the ships to strike targets in Japan in preparation for the

This Mark 8 range-keeping computer on BB-64 kept track of the many variables of gunfire: ship speed and bearing, wind speed, type of projectile, weight of gun charge, and target range, deflection, speed, and bearing.

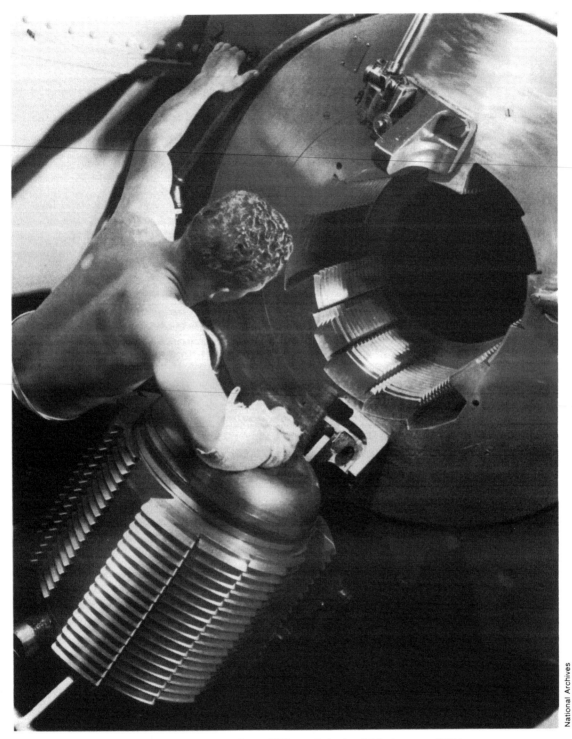

Gun captain at the open breech of one of Wisconsin's *nine 16-inch guns, off Okinawa, May, 1945. He is wiping the "mushroom" with a padded towel to ensure that no powder residue remains after firing.*

scheduled invasion of the home islands in the autumn of 1945. Halsey's fleet represented the greatest mass of sea power ever assembled.

The *Wisconsin* joined a striking force composed of the battleships *Iowa* and *Missouri*, two cruisers, and nine destroyers. On July 15, *Wisconsin* bombarded the Nippon Steel and Wanishi Iron Works at Muroran, Hokkaido. Opening at 32,000 yards and firing for forty minutes, *Wisconsin* expended 291 explosive 16-inch projectiles on the targets. Of the 900 heavy projectiles fired by the American battleships, 170 struck the plant, causing extensive damage.

Aiming the 16-inch main battery weapons required a sophisticated fire-control system. The equation for each salvo was different, and very complex. Calculations had to be made for the speed and direction of the ship as well as the direction of the target. Wind and weather conditions, the battleship's pitch and roll, the state and condition of each gun's bore, together with the curvature and rotation of the earth were among the numerous variables digested by two Mark 8 range-keeping computers. Range-finding directors determined target distances and bearings more accurately than the radar systems of the day. Gyroscopic devices stabilized the entire fire control system.

Hitting targets on land was never easy. In spite of their great inherent accuracy, it was difficult to assess precisely the effect of 16-inch gunfire on shore targets fifteen miles away. Low visibility prevented accurate spotting at Hokkaido. Captain Roper recommended a slower rate of fire with fewer guns per salvo so that the targets "will be less obscured with smoke."

Two days later *Wisconsin* shelled the Hitachi Engineering Works northeast of Tokyo. Accompanied by the *Iowa, Missouri, Alabama, North Carolina*, and the British battleship *King George V*, the ships blasted three factories at night using radar-controlled main battery firing techniques. No Japanese resistance was encountered.

Japan capitulated on August 15, after nuclear bombs had destroyed the cities of Hiroshima and Nagasaki. About 100 *Wisconsin* sailors and marines volunteered to become part of the landing party assigned to occupy the Yokosuka Naval Yard in Tokyo Bay. Lieutenant (j.g.) John Roberts of Longview, Texas, recalled the "eerie" feeling he experienced approaching the Japanese homeland as part of the first American occupying force. Nobody knew what to expect. Rough seas and windy and cold weather turned out to be the only

U.S. ships and aircraft on triumphant review in Tokyo bay, August, 1945. The battleship at left is the class leader, Iowa *(BB-61).*

problems. Japanese civilians behaved politely; the American invaders eagerly sought souvenirs.

Wisconsin dropped anchor in Tokyo Bay three days after the formal ceremony marking the end of World War II. "Laughter and smiles" marked the faces of battleship crew members on V-J Day. It was "a really happy hour," recalled one veteran. Seventeen-year-old Signalman Third Class Frederick C. Mauritson of San Antonio, Texas, perhaps expressed the feelings of others when he reflected, "serving aboard the battleship U.S.S. *Wisconsin* was the greatest experience of my life. The greatest thrill was the day I stood on the signal bridge . . . with battleflags flying as we entered victoriously into Tokyo Bay along with the greatest gathering of warships the world had ever seen."

Not one crewman had been lost or wounded. The *Wisconsin* had never been hit. The ship had steamed 105,831 miles since joining the Third Fleet, and Captain Roper's reports showed that *Wisconsin* consumed, on average, 199.6 gallons of fuel oil per mile. The ship's mess lavishly hosted repatriated Canadian and American prisoners of war while the dental and medical department rendered treatment to those in need. *Wisconsin* embarked homeward-bound G.I.s at Okinawa, delivering them safely on October 15. Navy officials awarded the ship five battle stars.

The *Wisconsin* received a hero's welcome when it passed under San Francisco's Golden Gate Bridge. Governor Goodland's commission awaited them. In an impressive ceremony, the commissioners presented the silver service

Captain John W. Roper, commander of the U.S.S. Wisconsin, *accepting presentation silver service from the people of Wisconsin, San Francisco, October 26, 1945. Lieutenant-Governor Oscar Rennebohm sits behind him.*

SHSW WHi(X3)24930

The Wisconsin *transits the Panama Canal in 1947, with a foot to spare on either side.*

from the first battleship *Wisconsin* to the new ship. On October 26, 1945, John Dickinson, chairman of the presentation committee, transferred the silver (which had been on display at the capitol) to Captain Roper. Lt.-Governor Oscar Rennebohm expressed his hope that in the future *Wisconsin* would become a "leading member of the armada of peace." He also noted the great interest Wisconsinites took in the battleship and how unselfishly Wisconsin's citizens had backed U.S. war efforts. Rennebohm observed that support for the Navy was particularly strong in the Badger State and that its own shipbuilding industry had constructed nearly 600 surface vessels and submarines during the conflict.

AT PEACE

WITH the exception of the four *Iowa*-class ships, American battleships were decommissioned or placed in reserve status after the war. Unfinished battleships were cancelled. Postwar operations consisted of training and diplomatic missions designed to demonstrate American interest in South America and in Europe. The *Wisconsin*, for instance, visited Chile, Peru, and Venezuela in late 1946, and the presidents of all three nations paid courtesy visits.

Naval Reserve training cruises occupied most of *Wisconsin*'s time at sea during 1947. Reservists became important components of U.S. naval forces because large numbers of veteran sailors had been discharged after the war, leaving the fleet with a shortage of experienced men. (*Wisconsin* operated with about 600 fewer crew members during the late 1940's than it had during the war.)

Captain John M. Higgins, a native of Madison, took command of the ship in mid-1947. The *Wisconsin* embarked on a midshipmen's training cruise to England, Scotland, and Norway shortly thereafter. Officers and crew faced "the most overwhelming hospitality" on their European visit, remembered Lt.-Commander Charles K. Duncan, *Wisconsin*'s Executive Officer. "I was given a social event schedule two inches thick." Duncan assigned groups of crewmen to each of the parties. Higgins and the ship's band attended a reception hosted by the U.S. Ambassador to Norway on July Fourth. "This does much to improve and maintain good relations," noted Captain Higgins.

Wisconsin was decommissioned in 1948, becoming part of the Atlantic Reserve Fleet based at Norfolk. The ship's silver service was sent back to Wisconsin for display at the state cen-

BB-64 off the coast of Korea, March, 1952. The links of the massive anchor chains weigh 120 pounds each.

tennial exhibit. E. R. Wendelberg of Milwaukee built a ten-foot scale model of *Wisconsin* to complement the display at the centennial. The model was subsequently acquired by the State Historical Society of Wisconsin and it became the centerpiece of a museum exhibit focusing on the famous battleship. Fleet Admiral William Leahy unveiled the new exhibit in August, 1950, when he visited the historical society in Madison.

POLICE ACTION

WHEN North Korean forces attacked South Korea in June, 1950, the United States quickly became involved in what government officials described as a "police action." The conflict, however, developed rapidly into an undeclared war of no small magnitude. The Korean War (1950–1953) was carried out under the aegis of the United Nations as an exercise in collective security. The United States supplied many of the armed forces and most of the firepower in what eventually became a long, bloody stalemate.

The U.S. Navy sent ships and planes to support the South Koreans and the United Nations land forces committed to their aid. North Korea had no air force and no navy. Neither the Soviet Union nor the People's Republic of China, North Korea's sponsors in aggression, interfered directly with U.S. naval operations.

All *Iowa*-class battleships participated in the Korean conflict. Their job was to blockade North Korea along with other naval units. They covered real or feigned troop landings; besieged important ports in North Korea such as Hungnam, Wonsan, and Songjin; supplied gunfire support for U.N. ground forces; and destroyed trains, trucks, bridges, and enemy troop concentrations all along the Korean coastline.

Governor Walter J. Kohler, members of the state's congressional delegation, and other officials were on hand for the *Wisconsin*'s recommissioning in early March, 1951. Governor Kohler displayed the ship's silver service during the ceremonies and members of several veterans' organizations participated in the event. The Navy sent aircraft to Madison and Milwaukee to transport members of the governor's party to Portsmouth, Virginia.

Forty-six-year-old Captain Thomas Burrowes assumed command of the battleship. Shakedown and training cruises to Scotland, Portugal, Nova Scotia, New York, and Cuba preceded the transiting of the Panama Canal and *Wisconsin*'s arrival in Japan. There, Vice Admiral H. M. Martin, commander of the Seventh Fleet, chose *Wisconsin* as his flagship. The battleship relieved *New Jersey* in late 1951.

The *Wisconsin*'s main battery—nine 16-inch guns—did yeoman service in the Korean War. Her lighter guns were also fired, particularly during nighttime harassing missions, but the big guns, and questions concerning their effectiveness, became the focus of attention.

Using air spotters to direct fire, *Wisconsin*'s first five 16-inch projectiles of the war destroyed a Russian tank and two artillery pieces. The ship's next three salvos destroyed a North Korean supply depot. Harassing fire from the secondary 5-inch weapons supported the First Marine Division and the South Korean I Corps at night. Bunkers, gun emplacements, and troop concentrations were "very effectively" eliminated by 16-inch gunfire, reported Captain Burrowes.

The *Wisconsin* ranged up the east coast of North Korea, taking up position in Wonsan Gulf in late December. Carrier planes and coordinated battleship gunfire destroyed rail yards, supply depots, and small boat concentrations. *Wisconsin* brought all of her guns to bear on Wonsan, firing 236 explosive 16-inch projectiles during two days. Battleship fire suppressed enemy antiaircraft guns and American carrier planes provided spotting assistance in return. "Highly gratifying" results were achieved, according to reports.

Francis Cardinal Spellman celebrated mass aboard the *Wisconsin* on December 28. The battleship replenished its ammunition and supplies in Japan immediately thereafter. When it returned to the war zone, South Korean President Syngman Rhee and his wife came aboard to present an award to Vice Admiral Martin.

Wisconsin went back to the Kasong area in early 1952, firing 420 16-inch projectiles during five days in January, shelling bunkers and supply depots. When hard-pressed South Korean troops radioed for assistance on one occasion, the battleship's main battery blanketed attacking enemy troops who were in the open. Eight 16-inch rounds brought "100% target coverage," according to official reports. Ap-

Crewmen cleaning one of Wisconsin's *big guns, February, 1952. The* Iowa-class *battleships fired more 16-inch ordnance in Korea than they did in World War II.*

preciative South Koreans provided the ship with close spotting near the target area.

American ships and planes did their best to dislocate North Korea's transportation system in order to halt the southward flow of Russian and Chinese military supplies. Bridges and rail-yards were hit frequently, and repaired just as frequently. Bridge-busting became a deadly art during the war. *Wisconsin* bombarded bridges at Kojo. Her guns dropped two spans of a rail-way bridge near Kosong using shipboard spot-ters. She bombarded the Hodo Pando railyards at Wonsan, sending 107 16-inch shells into a roundhouse, repair buildings, numerous rail cars, and a locomotive. The ship's air spotter radioed "this was by far the best shooting he had seen." *Wisconsin*'s gunners fired 535 16-inch projectiles during the last week of January alone.

The Hodo Pando rail facility came under bombardment again on February 3 when *Wisconsin* re-entered Wonsan Gulf. Captain Bur-rowes ordered all engines stopped at 8:15 A.M. to increase the accuracy of the battleship's fire. *Wisconsin* gunners sent 278 16-inch and 549 5-inch shells into the marshalling yards, railroad bridges, roundhouse, and boxcars. Poor visi-bility and lack of air spotting assistance, how-ever, prevented accurate damage assessments.

Marines and South Korean soldiers called on *Wisconsin* to shell enemy bunkers, command posts, and trenches near Kosong after the Hodo Pando strike. The ship's big guns scored fifteen hits on a railroad bridge at the end of February, dropping an entire span within two hours. Ac-tion Reports indicated that "excellent" results had been achieved against the bridge and a nearby shipyard.

High-level naval and governmental officials conferred aboard *Wisconsin* at the end of the month when Captain H. C. Bruton of Little Rock, Arkansas, took command of the ship. They discussed the battleship's next mission and probably assessed the role of battleship's main battery. Battleships required close spotting as-sistance to ensure accurate firing. *Wisconsin*'s commanding officer had requested that several propeller-driven carrier planes be assigned to act as gunnery spotters for the battleship and that pre- and post-strike photo reconnaissance missions be carried out to assess damage.

Navy officials, however, chose not to order carrier commanders to provide the special help requested by the battleship. Rather, carrier planes would provide air spotting only after carrying out their own missions. Although ad-vocates of the battleship argued that high ex-plosives could be delivered more accurately and economically by means of big guns than by air-craft, the Navy was committed to air power and refused to provide the *Wisconsin* with the kind of full-time aerial spotting it requested.

Wisconsin steamed into the waters of far northern Korea on March 15, 1952, taking up position off the Songjin-Chaho area. Songjin, an important and heavily defended railroad center close to the Russian border, was to be systematically bombarded for twelve hours. General Quarters sounded during a pre-dawn snow flurry. *Wisconsin* turned broadside to the shore about two miles from the coast and be-gan firing at 6:13 A.M. Fifteen 16-inch explosive projectiles undermined a railroad embankment

Officer of the Wisconsin *inspecting damage inflicted by enemy 152mm artillery shell off Sonjin, North Korea, March 15, 1952.*

National Archives

U.S.S. Wisconsin *off Korea in company with the heavy cruiser* St. Paul *(right) and destroyer* Irving Day Wiltsie *(left), February, 1952.*

causing "two major rock slides," burying 600 feet of track, and rendering hundreds of yards of trackage inoperable. Four main battery shells hit a locomotive and a troop train. The ship's helicopter flew gunfire spotting missions to assess damage.

Captain Bruton turned *Wisconsin's* 16-inch guns on a railroad bridge and tunnel at 8:48. Fifteen shots "pulverized" the tunnel, Bruton reported, undercutting fifty feet of track. Rock slides closed the bridge. Then the ship's anti-aircraft guns raked the area at close range.

Wisconsin next bombarded a railroad tunnel at Mayang Do Island. Forty-two 16-inch shells destroyed the tunnel and nearby tracks. Three projectiles penetrated the tunnel's thick concrete walls, detonating inside.

Wisconsin cruised the coastline, firing at targets as they presented themselves, for several more hours. Then, quite suddenly, the ship's immunity to enemy fire disappeared. North Korean artillerymen hidden in caves on the Yoktaeso-Ri peninsula several miles away opened up on the battleship at 3:38 P.M. The first enemy salvo landed 100 yards off *Wiscon-*

sin's port bow. Two more shells splashed near the starboard quarter. Three minutes later, a heavy shell struck *Wisconsin's* deck on the starboard side. Gunners Mate Second Class Thomas F. Jacobs of Highland Park, Michigan, was at his station when the shell hit the 40mm antiaircraft gun position mounted below his own. A "white puff" went up, Jacobs recalled, and moments later the snow on the deck turned red. Three men fell wounded, including Jacobs' best friend. The North Korean shell blew a 24-by-30-inch hole in the ship's deck before breaking up on its armor, causing "negligible damage."

The *Wisconsin* became "real busy" after coming under fire, recalled Jacobs. The cave shielding the North Korean shore battery was located and targeted. Nine 16-inch shells crashed out. Captain Bruton reported "scoring two direct hits." The battleship fired 152 16-inch shells that eventful day, along with 449 5-inch shells and 595 rounds from its 40mm antiaircraft guns. The North Korean shell caused *Wisconsin's* only battle damage in two wars.

Some naval authorities used *Wisconsin's* ex-

41

During her return voyage from Korea to the States, BB-64 displayed her graceful hull in the Navy's floating drydock at Guam.

perience off Songjin to demonstrate the effectiveness of 16-inch gunfire against shore facilities. *Wisconsin* so battered the Songjin-Chaho area that rail traffic ceased for nearly a week. The Songjin bombardment was probably as close as Americans ever came to interdicting North Korea's supply routes. Still, even though naval gunfire hampered and hurt North Korea's transportations system, it did not close it down.

The U.S. Marines in Korea frequently called on battleships like *Wisconsin* for heavy gunfire support. "We were never able to fire enough ammunition to suit the Marines," remembered Captain Bruton. Quartermaster Third Class Gerald Wiedenhoeft of Milwaukee recounted an experience he had that attested to the ship's role in combat support. During a leave in late 1952 he ran into an old high school friend who was a veteran with the First Marine Division. When Wiedenhoeft mentioned that he served aboard *Wisconsin*, the Marine "couldn't shake my hand enough."

The *Wisconsin* departed Korean waters in April, 1952, after being relieved by the *Iowa*. On its return voyage, the battleship stopped at Guam to test the Navy's huge new experimental floating drydock.

THE LAST BATTLESHIP

THE conclusion of the Korean War brought calls for military economy, and America's expensive battleships soon began to be decommissioned. High operating costs and their extensive manpower needs contributed to battleship retirements in the mid-1950's. One by one the *Iowa*-class ships were decommissioned. *Iowa* left active service in 1953, *Missouri* in 1955, *New Jersey* in 1957. The *Wisconsin* became the last battleship in U.S. service.

Wisconsin participated in training missions and naval exercises after the Korean War. She visited Scotland, France, Cuba, Norway, Brazil, Trinidad, Panama, Japan, Hong Kong, Haiti, Denmark, Mexico, and Colombia as well as New York and Norfolk between 1952 and 1956. Crew members holystoned the teak deck; fixed, polished, painted, and scraped; joined the battleship's baseball and basketball teams; and otherwise carried out routine duties.

As battleships declined in the eyes of naval authorities, they rose in the minds of the public. Large numbers of tourists visited *Wisconsin*, for instance, when the ship docked in New York in June, 1953. Huge crowds descended on the battleship when it revisited the nation's largest

42

city two years later. Captain G. S. Patrick was a guest on Ed Sullivan's *Toast of the Town* television show, and 14,000 people waited in line for the opportunity to come aboard the famous battleship. According to Captain Patrick's Visit Report, *Wisconsin*'s Marine detachment had to be called out to "restore order" when the gates opened and the crowd surged forward.

Wisconsin took part in the Navy's Joint Civilian Orientation Cruise off the Virginia coast on May 5, 1956. The next day, *Wisconsin* collided with the destroyer *Eaton* during a heavy fog. *Wisconsin*'s bow was crumpled. The *Eaton* was nearly cut in two and had to be towed back to port. Norfolk Naval Shipyard workers fitted a 120-ton, sixty-eight-foot bow section from the unfinished *Iowa*-class battleship *Kentucky* to *Wisconsin* in record time. *Wisconsin* was ready for service sixteen days later, and she departed for Spain on July 9.

Wisconsin cruised the Mediterranean in February of 1957, visiting Gibraltar, Turkey, Italy, and Spain. The battleship provided midshipmen with a summer cruise to Cuba and to Chile before being sent to participate in NATO exercises in European waters.

The inevitable took place in November, 1958. The last cruise of BB-64 ran from Norfolk to New York, and representatives of state government were embarked for the short voyage. Captain John O. Miner returned the battleship's silver service to state officials at the decommissioning ceremony in New York. Wisconsin Attorney General Stewart Honeck accepted the silver and spoke of the "nostalgia and melancholy" of the event. It was, Honeck observed, "the passing of an era." For the first time since 1895, the United States Navy was without a battleship.

THE END OF THE TRAIL?

REAR Admiral Chester C. Woods reflected on the passing of the battleship during his speech at *Wisconsin*'s decommissioning ceremony. He explained that carrier planes "doomed" battleships and that "the end of the trail" had come at last "for this magnificent breed of ship." *Iowa*, *Wisconsin*, and *New Jersey* found storage berths at Philadelphia, while *Missouri* was mothballed at Bremerton, Washington. All other battleships were sold or

U.S. Naval Institute

The Wisconsin's *crumpled bow, shortly after colliding with the destroyer* Eaton *in heavy fog, May 6, 1953.*

scrapped. Big guns had been replaced by airplanes.

Yet by the mid-1960's America was at war again, and it was not long before the limitations of air power were revealed in Vietnam. Sometimes planes could not operate during bad weather or at night. Aircraft costs and complexities escalated dramatically. Antiaircraft weapons became increasingly lethal in the missile age, as hundreds of pilots discovered. Air power could not always provide sustained, accurate, high-volume fire to support land forces. Long-range naval gunfire might still have a role in modern warfare.

Proponents of naval firepower encouraged the recommissioning of the *New Jersey* during 1967. The battleship received an "austere modernization," which in fact cost only as much as four modern aircraft. Parts for the *New Jersey* were cannibalized from *Iowa* and *Wisconsin*. American policy makers declared target-rich North Vietnam off limits in late 1968, however, and the *New Jersey* returned to the United States within a year. The U.S. Marines, as might be expected, supported the battleship's reappearance; but war-weary and cost-conscious Congressmen did not.

Navy officials began action to dispose of the *Iowa*-class ships in 1972. The *New Jersey* and *Missouri* were sought after as museums. (Indeed, *Missouri* had been attracting about 100,000 tourists per year at her berth in Washington state.) But *Iowa* and *Wisconsin* would have been scrapped had not Marine Corps spokesmen argued for the retention of all four as "instant sea-control ships." Feasibility studies conducted by the Navy further indicated that the battleships could be fitted with modern missile systems. Concussion and blast pressures generated by the 16-inch guns, studies showed, would not harm the high-tech modern electronics upon which the missiles depend.

The Naval Ship System Command recommended that the battleships be scrapped in 1974 despite the continued interest in the vessels by Marines and proponents of modernization. Chief of Naval Operations Admiral Elmo Zumwalt, who had served aboard *Wisconsin*, however, intervened to prevent the battleships from being disposed of. Zumwalt believed that the battleships' big guns might be needed to support amphibious operations in the future.

In 1977, inspection revealed that the *Iowa*s were in excellent shape and that their hulls, machinery, and guns had fifteen years of service life remaining. But antiquated living arrangements and outmoded electronics made them unfit for service. The survey team recommended that the battleships be stricken from the Navy list. But Marine Corps spokesmen successfully appealed the decision to Chief of Naval Operations, and one-time skipper of the *Iowa*, Admiral Jimmy Holloway. The Marines noted that the modern Navy had scant ability to provide gunfire support for landing forces. Other studies revealed that between 1941 and 1979, 85 per cent of the Navy's ordnance had been expended against land targets. For example, repeated air strikes on the Thanh Hoa bridge in North Vietnam cost fifty U.S. aircraft, even though it could have been destroyed by the 16-inch guns of a battleship in a matter of hours.

By 1980, world affairs had taken an ominous turn. The fall of the Shah and the rise of revolutionary religious fundamentalism in Iran, the seizure of American hostages in the Middle East, Soviet-sponsored revolutionary successes in Nicaragua and threats to other Central American countries, the Russian invasion of Afghanistan, and the launching of the Soviet nuclear-powered missile cruiser *Kirov*—the largest surface warship other than aircraft carriers built since World War II—naturally led to a review of American defense needs. Recommissioning all four *Iowa*-class battleships would rapidly increase American naval strength, argued Chief of Naval Operations Admiral Thomas B. Hayward to his supporters in Congress.

President Jimmy Carter opposed the reactivization of the battleships. He narrowly succeeded in causing the defeat of legislation designed to provide funding for the *Iowa*s in mid-1980. But Carter's victory proved short-lived.

President Ronald Reagan took office in 1981, promising to upgrade national defenses. Reagan appointed John Lehman as Secretary of the Navy, and shortly thereafter, Lehman began promoting the reactivization of the battleships. Congressional opponents included both liberals and conservatives who felt that the ships were too expensive or too old-fashioned. Naval consultants such as the former editor of *Jane's Fighting Ships* characterized the reactivization plans as "ridiculous," largely because of the problems of training crewmen and manning such large ships. On a somewhat less compelling note, the Kitsap County Historical Society in Washington opposed reactivating the *Missouri* because it would lose its major visitor attraction.

Secretary Lehman took the case for battleship reactivization to Congress and to the public. He and his supporters argued that modernized battleships could operate effectively with carriers on offensive missions anywhere they might be needed. Battleships could, furthermore, operate without air cover in certain areas of the Third World. They could provide gunfire support for amphibious operations as well as strike targets on hostile shores. They could refuel smaller ships, operate and refuel

BB-64 undergoing refitting in the Ingalls Shipyard at Pascagoula, Mississippi, 1987.

naval helicopters, and relieve carriers on extended deployments.

Defensively, battleships represented the best-protected type of surface ships in existence. The vulnerability of modern thin-skinned surface ships to sea-skimming missiles such as the Exocet was demonstrated in the Falklands War (1982) and the Persian Gulf. By comparison, battleships offered a high degree of security to their crews. The *Iowa*s are, of course, neither invulnerable nor unsinkable; but they are more damage-resistant than any other ships afloat, and they remain the fastest surface warships in the American Navy.

Congress approved reactivating the battleships in mid-1981. President Reagan attended *New Jersey*'s recommissioning in December. The *Iowa* underwent modernization between 1983 and 1985; the *Missouri* followed. BB-64, the *Wisconsin*, the last battleship, began its refit in 1986.

REACTIVIZATION

FOURTEEN tugboats pushed the *Wisconsin* from the Philadelphia Naval Yard's inactive ship facility to Pier Six in the industrial area on January 30, 1986. This 2,000-foot voyage marked

45

Wisconsin's first movement in twenty-nine years. Workers removed obsolete berthing equipment and made initial preparations to have the battleship ready for recommissioning. Debris from a minor electrical fire was cleared.

Ocean tugs then towed the ship to New Orleans in August, 1986, for dry docking at the Avondale Shipyards. About 1,000 shipyard employees reworked *Wisconsin*'s four eighteen-foot-diameter propellers and its 887-foot-long hull. The battleship was towed to Ingalls Shipyard in Pascagoula, Mississippi, in early 1987.

The modernization program will cost $385 million—about the same as a vulnerable missile frigate like the U.S.S. *Stark*. The upgraded battleship is to be air-conditioned. New bunking equipment will afford the 1,500 enlisted crewmen privacy and reading lights. Vending machines will supplement an improved messing facility. Anti-pollution sewerage and garbage-disposal units bring the vessel into compliance with modern environmental standards, as will the conversion from World War II-era black oil to light distillate fuel. *Wisconsin*'s four engines and eight boilers are to be overhauled.

The modernization program will significantly improve the ship's weapons and electronics. State-of-the-art communications equipment, air and surface search radars, electronic countermeasure systems, and a helicopter aviation facility will enhance *Wisconsin*'s all-weather capabilities. New weapons will include the installation of thirty-two Tomahawk cruise missiles in eight armored box launchers. The Tomahawk can deliver a conventional or nuclear-tipped warhead up to 1,500 miles and strike within ten yards of a sea or land target. Sixteen Harpoon anti-ship missiles in four launchers will be added. The Harpoon carries its 570-pound conventional warhead sixty miles just above the wavetops before popping up as it nears the target to make a final steep diving attack.

Anti-missile defenses have also been added. Four Phalanx close-in weapons systems can deliver a very high volume of accurate light cannon fire against incoming missiles. The six-barreled Phalanx unleashes 3,000 rounds per minute (fifty per second). Each Phalanx has its own independent search-and-track radar system.

The *Wisconsin* lost all its light antiaircraft guns and eight of its dual-purpose 5-inch guns. Twelve 5-inch guns remain, however, and all nine of the great 16-inch guns have been retained. Moreover, gun systems will be improved. The introduction of special "Navy cool" powder and the addition of titanium dioxide and wax to existing propellants dramatically reduces bore erosion in the 16-inch guns, thereby prolonging barrel life. Rocket-assisted projectile experiments are being carried out now and they are expected to extend the range of both the 5-inch and 16-inch guns. Infra-red and laser homing guidance systems will improve the accuracy of the guns. Thus modernized and upgraded, the *Wisconsin* will constitute a formidable weapon of naval strategy and a force in international diplomacy.

RECOMMISSIONING

STATE officials became involved in *Wisconsin*'s recommissioning during 1987 when Governor Tommy G. Thompson signed an executive order creating a commission to coordinate public awareness about the ship and interact with Navy representatives. *Wisconsin*'s forty-eight-piece silver service was again made available to the ship. James McVey, president of Oscar Mayer Foods and himself a Navy veteran, became head of the governor's commission in April.

Governor Thompson's enthusiasm for the recommissioning of the *Wisconsin* was contagious. Several hundred people, including private citizens, legislators, and other state officials, volunteered for the commission. "I have never received more requests to serve on a commission," an obviously pleased governor reported. The battleship commission will sponsor a festive celebration in October, 1988, when *Wisconsin* is recommissioned at Pascagoula. Several hundred veterans of *Wisconsin* are anticipated for a reunion along with thousands of state citizens. "We are going to do it up right," Governor Thompson said of the celebration.

State Historical Society of Wisconsin Director H. Nicholas Muller III directed his staff to mark the recommissioning of the battleship by preparing exhibits and publishing a commemorative history. A major display on the ship is

SHSW WHi(X3)44263

*Shipboard display case containing the ship's presentation silver, c. 1957. An essay on
the silver service follows this brief history of the battleships* Wisconsin.

to open at the new state museum during August, 1988, where artifacts donated by the Navy, including the *Wisconsin*'s bell, will be featured. Traveling exhibits were made available in time to celebrate Armed Forces Day in Milwaukee.

The *Wisconsin*'s new skipper, Captain Jerry M. Blesch of Fort Thomas, Kentucky, attended an impressive ceremony in the state capitol where Governor Thompson inducted seventy-eight young Wisconsin men into a special contingent of enlisted personnel into the Navy in February, 1988. They became part of the battleship's crew. In short, the state took an active and immediate interest in the recommissioning of its namesake ship. The relationship between the U.S.S. *Wisconsin* and the state of Wisconsin will continue after the recommissioning cele-

bration, as the governor's commission produced a documentary video and sponsored a speakers' bureau for long-term educational purposes.

RETROSPECTIVE

THE *Wisconsin* and the other *Iowa*-class battleships are the most beautiful and puzzling capital ships of the World War II era. *Wisconsin* was never tested in action against the enemy battleships it was designed to fight. It entered service too late, and airplanes had become the Navy's primary weapon. The remarkably high speed of the *Iowa*s made them ideal companions for the fast aircraft carriers, however, and for that reason they remained in service long

Official U.S. Navy photo

Captain Jerry M. Blesch, USN, commanding officer of the recommissioned U.S.S. Wisconsin, *1987.*

after all other battleships were scrapped. U.S. battleship designers had emphasized staying power over speed since the 1890's. Yet the *Iowas* departed from traditional American practice by favoring speed over other important characteristics. Thus, the world's only operational battleships are themselves uniquely unrepresentative vessels.

As America's global troubleshooters, the U.S. Marines have come to prize the big-gun ships and have argued persuasively for their retention. (On the other hand, the Marines would likely be just as pleased with any old barge so long as it mounted 16-inch guns!) Another ar-

gument for the battleship is the relative economy of its weaponry. For example, seven salvos from *Wisconsin's* nine 16-inch guns equal the payload carried by sixty carrier-borne aircraft—and at one-twelfth the cost. *Wisconsin* can deliver 210 tons of high explosives within eighty minutes under any weather conditions; carrier planes require decent weather, twelve hours, and three separate air strikes to do the same job. To be sure, the aircraft have a much longer range than the ship's main battery; but the crewman aboard a fast armored vessel is intrinsically safer in combat than the pilot of a jet aircraft.

And so the debate continues. Given that an old-fashioned surface engagement between the major sea powers is highly unlikely, the question remains: What is the role of the fast battleship in the final decades of the twentieth century? In this age of violent "peace," do America's four battlewagons comprise a credible military and diplomatic force in world affairs? Does the recommissioned *Wisconsin* represent a white elephant, a sitting duck, or a powerful and highly mobile peacekeeping weapon? There is no doubt about the ability of a battleship to impress with its sheer size and majesty. Better than any submarine or lesser vessel, it can "show the flag" and impart a sense of American strength and resolve. But will that be enough to justify the high cost of crewing and maintaining it forty years after it was pronounced obsolete?

None of these legitimate concerns detracts from the importance of the U.S.S. *Wisconsin* or its recommissioning. With her sister ships, *Wisconsin* was and remains an impressive example of naval technology and design. She is beautiful, long-lived, and, as the last of her kind, historically unique. As she enters this final stage of her long career, she remains the embodiment of American sea power.

The U.S.S. *Wisconsin* Silver Service

By Anne Woodhouse

CURATOR OF DECORATIVE ARTS
STATE HISTORICAL SOCIETY OF WISCONSIN

SILVER has long been made into special pieces to celebrate, congratulate, or commemorate. Several factors combined to make the late nineteenth and early twentieth centuries the heyday of formal presentation silver. Great lodes of silver were discovered in the western United States, making possible the fashioning of large and impressive pieces. Silversmithing firms grew into silver-manufacturing concerns, capable of producing services consisting of dozens of pieces. The emergence of the United States as a world power with an impressive naval force was achieved during the final years of the century. The desire to represent the nation with suitable ceremony on formal occasions was an outgrowth of national and state pride in our accomplishments.

American battleships are traditionally named for states of the Union; cruisers, for cities. The custom of a state or city presenting a silver service to a naval vessel bearing its name began in earnest in the early 1890's. Between 1891 and 1907, the Gorham Company of Providence, Rhode Island, alone made more than two dozen such services. After World War I,

the tradition slowed to a trickle. The presentation custom was never obligatory, so some vessels do not have silver services.[1]

The U.S.S. *Wisconsin* silver was made in two stages. The first set, voted by unanimous action of the state legislature in 1899, falls squarely in the center of the major period of activity for ordering battleship silver services. Though few services were being made during the Second World War, Wisconsinites' pride in the building of a new namesake battleship led in 1943 to the authorization of money to refurbish and augment the first set.

State commissions were set up to plan the commissioning ceremonies of both the first and second battleships *Wisconsin*. Their duties included the ordering of the silver. The contract for providing a battleship silver service was typically awarded to a jewelry firm within the state, which subcontracted in turn to a large silver-manufacturing company, which actually made the pieces. Both commissions chose Milwaukee businesses to be their agents. In 1899, the winner of the contract was the C. Preusser Jewelry Company on Water Street, which was in business from about 1880 to 1910. In 1943, the contract was awarded to Schwanke-Kasten, suc-

I wish to thank the following for their help with the research and preparation of this essay: Fred Roy, Jr., Director of Design for Gorham; David Rogers, Manager of Design-Hollowware at Gorham; Sam Hough, cataloger of the Gorham archives at the John Hay Library, Brown University; Ann Wood, Curatorial Assistant, The Museum of Fine Arts, Houston; James Mitchell, Curator of Industry and Technology, William Penn Memorial Museum; Cdr. Jeff Renard, USN; Lt. Terri Kaisch, USN; and Captain Jerry M. Blesch, USN.

[1] A recent exhibit and catalog deal with presentation silver: *Marks of Achievement: Four Centuries of American Presentation Silver*, by the staff of The Museum of Fine Arts, Houston (New York, 1987). This is one of the few attempts to deal with the subject of battleship silver. Information on Gorham, in addition to that shared by the staff, can be found in Charles H. Carpenter, Jr., *Gorham Silver 1831–1981* (New York, 1982).

The punch bowl's function is implied by the grapes which form its rim. A pair of badgers are perched on cornucopia-shaped handles overflowing with Wisconsin wheat and pine, a motif which is repeated on the cups.

cessor in 1937 to the firm of Alsted-Kasten, co-founded in 1899 by Charles Kasten, former vice-president of C. Preusser. (Schwanke-Kasten is still thriving, and one of its staff, William Dixon, serves on the current governor's commission.)

The chosen firm in each case was responsible for acting as liaison between the state and the manufacturing firm, for selecting and ordering the pieces, for marking them with the firm's name as retailer, and for handling the payment. The silver-manufacturing firm chosen to make both sets was the Gorham Company of Providence. Gorham made more silver for naval vessels than any other company; a service it made in 1961 for the cruiser *Long Beach* was its sixty-first.

Gorham made thirty-five pieces in the first service for the U.S.S. *Wisconsin.* They were a twenty-six-inch oval and a twenty-two-inch round tray or "waiter"; a pair of candelabra, each holding seven candles; two punch bowls and ladles; twenty-four punch cups; a fruit dish; a compote; and an elaborate centerpiece with four dishes for fruit or flowers attached to the corners. The service contained a total of 1,552 ounces of silver.

Placed aboard the U.S.S. *Wisconsin* shortly after its commissioning in 1901, the set was used for formal receptions until BB-9 was decommissioned in 1920. As it was customary for silver without a ship to be placed aboard a ship without silver, the service was subsequently used aboard the carrier *Yorktown* before being stored by the Navy in San Diego. When the second *Wisconsin* was under construction in 1943, Governor Walter S. Goodland appointed John Dickinson head of a committee to oversee the refurbishment and augmentation of the old service. The legislature appropriated $7,500 for this purpose. The Milwaukee firm of Schwanke-Kasten was chosen to be agent for the refurbishing and the ordering of the new tea and coffee services. William Schwanke co-ordinated the ordering and the selection of Gorham, acting as liaison with the presentation committee. A few pieces needed replacement, and a decision was made to add a tea and coffee service, perhaps reflecting a desire to entertain smaller groups of people. Gorham was chosen to refurbish the old set and produce the new pieces. The work had to take second place to the production of war materials, of course, for skilled craftsmen during wartime were expected to use their talents in the making of precision instruments; but Gorham's vice-president promised that this phase of the work could be completed in three months.[2]

Pieces which needed replacement were the four centerpiece branches, one punch cup, and one ladle. The compote from the first set was duplicated. The new pieces were a coffee pot, teapot, and hot water kettle on a stand with an alcohol burner; a sugar bowl; a cream pitcher; a waste bowl; and a thirty-two-inch tray or waiter. Not only did Gorham still have the original casting patterns, but some of the craftsmen who had made the original set may well have also worked on the additional pieces.[3]

The refurbished first set of silver was symbolically presented to the people of Wisconsin in the assembly chamber of the state capitol on May 29, 1943. Admiral William Leahy made the presentation, and Governor Goodland accepted the service on behalf of the people of Wisconsin. Many more Wisconsin citizens were able to see the silver when it was displayed in the lobby of the Milwaukee *Journal* building in 1944 and in the windows of Schwanke-Kasten in 1945. (Silver services are removed from vessels in time of war, so the *Wisconsin* silver was displayed temporarily in Governor Goodland's executive reception room pending the selection of a date for the presentation.)

Members of the committee for the presentation traveled to San Francisco for the ceremony, which took place on October 26, 1945. John Dickinson spoke first, followed by William Schwanke, who gave a history of the silver service. The formal presentation was made by Chief Justice Marvin Rosenberry, representing Governor Goodland. Captain John Roper accepted the service on behalf of the Navy. "On,

Wisconsin" was played and naval planes flew overhead.

With the decommissioning of the *Wisconsin* in 1948, the silver service became available to be displayed in Wisconsin for the state centennial celebration. It was then returned to the Navy to be carried on the carrier U.S.S. *Coral Sea*. When the *Wisconsin* was recommissioned on March 3, 1951, the silver was reassigned to the ship, though it would not have been aboard during action in the Korean War.

After the *Wisconsin*'s decommissioning in 1958, the service was displayed in the lobby of the State Historical Society of Wisconsin in Madison. Since that time it has been used occasionally for official state and university functions.

The *Wisconsin* service was neither the simplest nor the most elaborate battleship service made. A 1907 Navy report listing gifts to naval vessels includes several more modest presen-

Naval and nautical symbols are plentiful on the candelabra. Dolphins support the branches, sea shells and seaweed ornament the candle cups, and (on the central shaft) an American eagle grasps an anchor.

[2]Information contained in a letter from Gorham Vice-President William F. McChesney to William Schwanke of Schwanke-Kasten, undated (before August 25, 1943). Typed copy in Wisconsin State Archives, Records of the Office of the Governor, Wisconsin silver correspondence, Series 144.

[3]"Well Done U.S.S. Wisconsin," by Edward N. Doan, an article in the Wisconsin *Blue Book* of 1946, covers the 1940's history of ship and silver. This citation is from p. 186: "Some of the same craftsmen who had hammered the designs into the original service worked on the new pieces," but no specific craftsmen are named.

tations of loving cups and punch bowls.[4] At the other extreme, the battleship *Pennsylvania*'s 162 pieces, made just a few years later, included a smoking set, an ice-cream set, and an extremely elaborate centerpiece combining a bowl for fruit or flowers with ten candelabra branches which were fitted with electrified candles and shades. Decoration included relief motifs of oil wells, steel mills, and a chased depiction of Benjamin West's painting of William Penn's treaty with the Indians.[5]

Some of the smaller pieces in the *Wisconsin* set seem to have been adapted from standard Gorham shapes, but the larger pieces were specially designed. The decoration of the service reflects the symbols and resources of the state. Pine cones and branches, sheaves of wheat, cavorting badgers, and a scene of Indians harvesting wild rice supplement the state seal on the larger pieces. Nautical symbolism includes dolphins, seashells, a crowned figure probably representing Neptune, and the seal of the United States Navy.

The Wisconsin pieces are molded in heavy relief and the sculptural quality is heightened by an oxidation of the lower areas to give a greater sense of depth. The style of the set has often been called "late Georgian," although the late nineteenth century was a period of great eclecticism during which many earlier styles were revived and adapted. A recent book about Gorham silver describes the trend as "Academic Design," a counterpart of the Beaux-Arts movement in architecture.[6] Elements of Art Nouveau can also be discerned, particularly in the sinuous lines on the rims of the punch bowls, centerpiece, and fruit bowl.

A salesman's manual put out by Gorham in the 1930's described the value of silver articles as dependent on design, execution, weight, and finish, and stated that knowledge of construction was essential to understand and explain silver. The descriptions of processes in this manual are still used by the company's director of design to answer questions about Gorham's practices, and the techniques covered would have been the same for making both sets.[7]

[4]Report of the Secretary of the Navy, in *Annual Reports of the Navy Department for the Fiscal Year 1907* (Washington, 1908), Appendix A, p. 42.
[5]*The Silver Service of the U.S.S. Pennsylvania* (Harrisburg, 1981).

[6]Carpenter, *Gorham Silver*, p. 12.
[7]"The Sales Manual and History of the Gorham Company, published at Providence February First 1932," is a typed salesman's manual and production description.

This scene of Indian women harvesting wild rice was adapted for the punch bowl from an original work by Seth Eastman, reproduced in engraved form in Henry Rowe School-craft's Indian Tribes of the United States. *Note the state motto, "Forward," above the Navy seal.*

Harper-Fritsch Studios

This detail of the candelabra reveals the fineness of detail produced by Gorham's crafts-men. Shells, seaweed, and the head of Neptune are flanked by a pair of Wisconsin badgers.

Craftsmen at Gorham still undergo a five-year apprenticeship. This develops skill in a particular area and ensures a basic familiarity with the whole manufacturing process. Chasing, engraving, and silversmithing are examples of specialization in the craft. Highly skilled craftsmen performed a great deal of hand work, making battleship services some of the most impressive silver ever produced.

Forming of the pieces required different techniques according to the type of piece. To make the trays, blueprints were made from the design drawings. The blueprint was then laid on a piece of sheet silver and the design and outline transferred by scratching or pricking through the blueprint with an awl-like tool and powdered chalk. The piece was cut from the blank sheet of silver with a jewelers' saw or band saw and the design formed by hand raising.

Pieces such as the coffee and teapots, pitcher, sugar bowl, waste bowl, and punch bowls were formed by another process called spinning. This involves placing the silver sheet on a hardwood or steel form, or chuck, and turning the chuck on a lathe, pressing against the silver with a steel tool to make the silver conform to the shape of the chuck. Another operation performed in the spinning department was the turning over of edges.

The two ladles for punch were the only items in the service which are part of the category called flatware, a term which usually applies to knives, forks, spoons, and food serving pieces. (All the other pieces in the set are considered "hollowware.") The bulk of Gorham's business still comes from flatware, made in many different patterns. These ladles were probably standard Gorham items since they bear no Wisconsin-related decoration and cost only $40 and $45. Their elaborate handles were formed by casting. The candelabra also required extensive use of the casting technique, not only for the branches and the applied cast badgers, but for the body of each piece as well. Casting, the forming of liquid metal either in a mold or through the lost-wax process, results in a more porous metal with a grayish or bluish appearance. (The candelabra do, in fact, seem to be a slightly different color from the rest of the service.)

The seal of the State of Wisconsin is a special

feature on many of the pieces and was also formed by casting. To make the original casting pattern, a model was made three times life size in clay and plaster to get the detail, then reduced to life size using a pantograph. While the stylus traced the master, an attached cutter bit into a bronze blank. The detail was sharpened by chasing. Gorham still owns the casting pattern for the Wisconsin seal as well as the standard casting patterns used for other elements.

After the special-order pieces received their basic form, they had components such as finials, spouts, and branches attached in the silversmithing department. This operation was done with a solder of 75 per cent fine silver and 25 per cent copper and zinc in equal amounts. This combination produced a lasting solder with a high melting point. Also in this department, the edges of the pieces would be filed and cast borders applied. The punch bowls and centerpiece are good examples of pieces with cast applied borders.

Once the pieces had been assembled, it was time to add the ornament. Chasing was the most important technique used on the *Wisconsin* silver. The section on chasing from the Gorham manual conveys a sense of the complex process: "In this department decoration is placed on the finished product by chasing, which consists of hammering a blunt tool against the metal. The two types of chasing are flat and repoussé. The latter differs in that the metal is raised from the inside or reverse side. This is accomplished by means of a snarling iron. This iron is supported in a vice and the article . . . to be chased . . . is placed over the upturned point. The part at which the ornament is to stand out in relief is rested on the point and the iron is hammered. The vibration of the snarling iron bumps up the metal. The ornament is then chased in the elevated section and any of the elevation not decorated is carefully pounded back leaving the ornament in relief. Hundreds of tools, varying in size and shape, are employed by a chaser which are fashioned by himself."[8]

The punch bowls and centerpiece have been extensively decorated using the repoussé chasing technique; this is what forms most of the special Wisconsin motifs such as pine boughs and sheaves of wheat.

Both punch bowls also bear the engraved message "From the people of Wisconsin by unanimous vote of the legislature, 1899." This was engraved, a technique that differs from chasing in that the silver is cut away in a fine line rather than pounded down. The scene on one punch bowl of Indians harvesting wild rice was also engraved.

Once the pieces were completed, they had scratches and file marks removed with pumice, oil, and a walrus hide buffer or hair brush. The bottoms of the trays had hammer marks removed with pumice stone. The surface of the parts with deep relief was then oxidized to blacken the lower areas, resulting in an increased contrast between upper and lower parts of the design. Some of the pieces were subsequently gilded on the inside.

The last operation was the finishing process. Gorham described the treatment chosen for the *Wisconsin* silver as a "soft French grey finish," very similar to the "butler finish" Gorham uses today. The polish consisted of a fine volcanic dust in a base of stearic acid and vaseline. The polishing causes thousands of minute scratches which produce a soft, mellow glow.

American silver is almost always marked, a custom which makes identifying and tracing its history possible. The *Wisconsin* silver service bears several different marks on the base of the pieces. These marks are useful for verifying the maker, date, and sometimes extra information. The retailers' marks—"C. Preusser Jewelry Co." for the earlier set, "Schwanke-Kasten Co. Jewelers Milwaukee" for the later—make it easy to tell which pieces were made for each set. This is especially helpful information to identify the replacement pieces. Gorham silver is marked with the firm's name in capital letters and three small stamps depicting a lion, an anchor, and a Gothic "G." The earlier set was given the order numbers 9666 through 9676, which appear within a rectangle indicating that this was a special-order set. A stamped sickle shape on the base of one piece, Gorham's symbol for 1899, proves that it was made in the year the legislative appropriation was made and the order was placed.

By the 1940's, the marking system had

[8]*Ibid.*, p. 86.

changed. Most of the set was identified by the letters JEU, with JEV for the kettle and JEW for the waiter. The date was shown by a square, indicating the fourth decade of the twentieth century, enclosing a 4, meaning the fourth year of that decade: 1944.

Both sets are stamped "sterling." This is an English term for a standard of 925 parts silver per thousand. Pure silver is too soft to maintain its shape during hard use, so it is commonly alloyed with 75 parts per thousand of copper to harden it. Sterling is thus 92.5 per cent pure silver.

With the recommissioning of the *Wisconsin* in 1988, the opportunity has once more arisen to display and use a portion of the silver service aboard ship. When the ship is in port, the entertainment of local dignitaries and govern-ment leaders calls for a suitable setting and an impressive and beautiful silver service. The silver will reflect the pride of the citizens of Wisconsin in the ship which bears the state name, and will also continue a historical connection between Wisconsinites and their battleship dating back to the turn of the century. As Captain Jerry M. Blesch has remarked on the continuance of this tradition: "We will be proud to use the magnificent silver service at appropriate official functions around the world. At other times, the silver can be viewed in the wardroom in a secure display case. The citizens of Wisconsin will always be welcome aboard to visit and view their beautiful gift."[9]

[9]Telephone conversation with Commander Jeff Renard, March 2, 1988.

Harper-Fritsch Studios

A tea and coffee service was added to the Wisconsin's *silver in the 1940's. The Gorham Company (now a division of Textron, Inc.) still has the blueprints used in making this set, as well as original drawings for the tray and coffee pot.*

FOR FURTHER READING

Historical literature abounds with works on battleships. The following are books that can be obtained with relative ease from a good general library.

Starting from the present battleship era and working backward in terms of historical time, valuable and interesting information is presented in Malcom Muir's excellent book, *The Iowa Class Battleships* (Dorset, United Kingdom, 1987), which focuses exclusively on the history and development of the four *Iowas*. It is profusely illustrated and extremely well written. Robert O. Dulin and Robert Gartzke's *U.S. Battleships in World War II* (Annapolis, 1976) is a comprehensive work on the history of American battleships during the war era. Both volumes of the Squadron/Signal Publications, *U.S. Battleships in Action* (Carrollton, Texas, 1980–1984), by Robert C. Stern, are excellent. *U.S. Battleships: An Illustrated Design History* (Annapolis, 1985), by Norman Friedman, is a very thorough and technically oriented book intended primarily for specialists, as is Siegfried Byer's *Battleships and Battle Cruisers, 1905–1970: Historical Development of the Capital Ship* (Garden City, 1973).

Older battleships, such as the first *Wisconsin*, are described and analyzed by John C. Reilly, Jr., and Robert L. Scheina in *American Battleships, 1886–1923: Pre-Dreadnought Design and Construction* (Annapolis, 1980). Brayton Harris' *The Age of the Battleship, 1890–1922* (New York, 1965), and Walter R. Herrick's *The American Naval Revolution* (Baton Rouge, 1967), review the meteoric rise of the New Navy and the importance of battleships to that important chapter of American history. Robert A. Hart discusses one of the most dramatic episodes in battleship history in his well-written book *The Great White Fleet* (Boston, 1965).

For Civil War buffs and aficionados of the age of steam and iron, Frank M. Bennett's two-volume classic, *The Steam Navy of the United States* (Pittsburgh, 1897), is now available as a reprint. J. P. Baxter's *Introduction of the Ironclad Warship* (Cambridge, United Kingdom, 1933), and Sir Reginald Custance's *The Ship of the Line in Battle* (Edinburgh, Scotland, 1912), likewise provide great reading for those interested in the topic of early ironclads. *The Navy in the Civil War* series, published by Charles Scribner and Sons during the 1880's, features two highly readable accounts of ironclads in action. These include Daniel Ammen's *The Atlantic Coast* (New York, 1883), and *The Gulf and Inland Waters* (New York, 1883), by none other than Alfred Thayer Mahan—the prophet of battleships.

General naval histories are invaluable for gaining an understanding of world events and the role that battleships played in them. Harold and Margaret Sprout wrote one of the best overview accounts in *The Rise of American Naval Power, 1776–1918* (Princeton, 1939). It has been updated several times and became available as a paperback in 1966. Samuel Eliot Morison's fifteen-volume *History of United States Naval Operations in World War II* (Boston, 1947–1962) has yet to be improved upon. James A. Field's *History of U.S. Naval Operations: Korea* (Washington, 1962) is adequate and can be supplemented by Malcom W. Cagle and Frank A. Manson's *The Sea War in Korea* (Annapolis, 1957). Edward L. Beach's *The United States Navy: A 200 Year History* (Boston, 1986) provides a modest general survey.